荆楚理工学院校级科研项目"顺应论视角下的法律文本翻译研究"（QN201611）
湖北省教育科学"十二五"规划重点课题"转型背景下地方本科院校商务英语专业应用型人才培养模式研究"（2014A038）

ENGLISH FOR IMPORT AND EXPORT PRACTICES

王娇艳 编著

中国地质大学出版社
ZHONGGUO DIZHI DAXUE CHUBANSHE

图书在版编目(CIP)数据

English for Import and Export Practices/王娇艳编著. —武汉：中国地质大学出版社，2016.8
ISBN 978-7-5625-3870-7

Ⅰ.①E…
Ⅱ.①王…
Ⅲ.①进出口贸易-贸易实务
Ⅳ.①F740.4

中国版本图书馆 CIP 数据核字(2016)第 228519 号

English for Import and Export Practices	王娇艳　编著
责任编辑：段连秀　　策划编辑：叶友志　张　华　　责任校对：张咏梅	
出版发行：中国地质大学出版社(武汉市洪山区鲁磨路 388 号)　　邮政编码：430074	
电　　话：(027)67883511　　传真：67883580　　E-mail:cbb@cug.edu.cn	
经　　销：全国新华书店　　　　　　　　　　　　http://www.cugp.cug.edu.cn	
开本：787 毫米×960 毫米 1/16	字数：400 千字　　印张：12.75
版次：2016 年 8 月第 1 版	印次：2016 年 8 月第 1 次印刷
印刷：武汉教文印刷厂	印数：1—500 册
ISBN 978-7-5625-3870-7	定价：48.00 元

如有印装质量问题请与印刷厂联系调换

前 言

　　国际贸易作为国际商务的最主要的组成部分，涉及商品进出口、货物运输、货物保险、国际支付等方面，因此，除了具备良好的外语能力，还必须掌握与国际经济贸易有关的专业知识。本书结合国际贸易中不断出现的新现象，参考了国内外最新修订、公布的有关法规和国际贸易的惯例和规则，体现了适时、适度和适用的原则。本书包括了国际贸易最主要的内容，各章节体现了出口贸易流程，在编写中重点突出实践环节的实务讲解，在每一章都有知识点聚焦，以帮助读者构建知识框架，在学习时能明确学习的目的和重难点所在，具体重难点穿插案例分析和讨论。另外，为了巩固每一章的学习内容，在每一章后面增加了针对性的练习题和案例分析，同时还增加了UCP600相应条款的介绍，以帮助读者将知识融会贯通，了解国际惯例。

　　本书可作为高校涉外专业学习专业英语的教材，也可供从事国际贸易工作的人员学习参考。由于编者水平和时间有限，错误难免，敬请专家、读者批评指正。

作　者

2016 年 7 月

Contents

Chapter 1　General Introduction ·· (1)

1.1　Export Procedure ··· (1)

1.2　Organizations Involved in Export Trade ································· (4)

1.3　Documents Involved in Export Trade ······································ (5)

Chapter 2　Preparation ·· (6)

2.1　Market Research and Promotion ··· (6)

2.2　Establishing Trade Relations ·· (7)

Exercise ·· (11)

Chapter 3　Business Negotiation ··· (15)

3.1　Inquiry ·· (15)

3.2　Offer ··· (16)

3.3　Counter-offer ··· (20)

3.4　Acceptance ·· (21)

3.5　Contract ·· (22)

Exercise ·· (38)

Chapter 4　Quality, Quantity and Packing of Goods ···················· (43)

4.1　Ways of Expressing Quality ··· (43)

4.2　Quantity ·· (46)

4.3　Packing ··· (48)

Exercise ·· (49)

Chapter 5　Incoterms ··· (54)

5.1　Functions of Trade Terms ··· (54)

5.2　Terms for Any Mode of Transport ··· (55)

5.3　Terms for Sea and Inland Waterway Transport ······················ (69)

5.4　Calculation of Quotation ··· (88)

Exercise ·· (90)

III

Chapter 6 Ocean Transport .... (93)

6.1 Ocean Transport .... (93)
6.2 Shipment Clause in Contract .... (94)
6.3 Bill of Lading .... (95)
Exercise .... (106)

Chapter 7 Insurance .... (110)

7.1 Risks, Losses and Expenses .... (110)
7.2 Coverages under CIC .... (113)
7.3 W/W Clause (commencement and termination of the insurance) ... (115)
7.4 Insurance Clause in Contract .... (116)
7.5 Insurance Policy .... (117)
Exercise .... (121)

Chapter 8 Payment .... (128)

8.1 Lead in Practice .... (128)
8.2 Means of Payment .... (129)
8.3 Modes of Payment .... (134)
Exercise .... (155)

Chapter 9 Documents .... (166)

9.1 Commercial Invoice .... (166)
9.2 Certificate of Origin Form A .... (168)
9.3 Ocean Bill of Lading .... (169)
9.4 Insurance Policy .... (170)

Chapter 10 Claims and Arbitration .... (175)

10.1 Breach of Contract .... (175)
10.2 Claim .... (176)
10.3 Force Majeure .... (177)
10.4 Arbitration .... (178)
Exercise .... (185)

Glossary .... (187)

Reference to Exercise .... (189)

Chapter 1　General Introduction

Export procedure
Organizations involved in export trade
Documents involved in export trade

Import and export are subject to a lot of formalities, such as customs entry and exchange control approval. This means that the procedure of foreign trade is more complicated than that of domestic trade. This chapter tries to present a general picture and a brief introduction to export and import trade for the purpose of clarifying their complicated procedures.

1.1　Export Procedure

From the very beginning to the end of a transaction, the whole operation generally goes through four stages: preparation for export, business negotiation, implementation of contract and settlement of disputes (if any). Since the export and import trades are two sides and opposite to each other, we will take the procedure of export trade to illustrate the general procedures of export and import transaction.

1.1.1　Preparation for export

Preparation starts from doing market research which covers research on the importing country or regions, research on the market and research on the customer. The exporter should know the political, financial and economic conditions in the importing country, investigate their laws, regulations governing

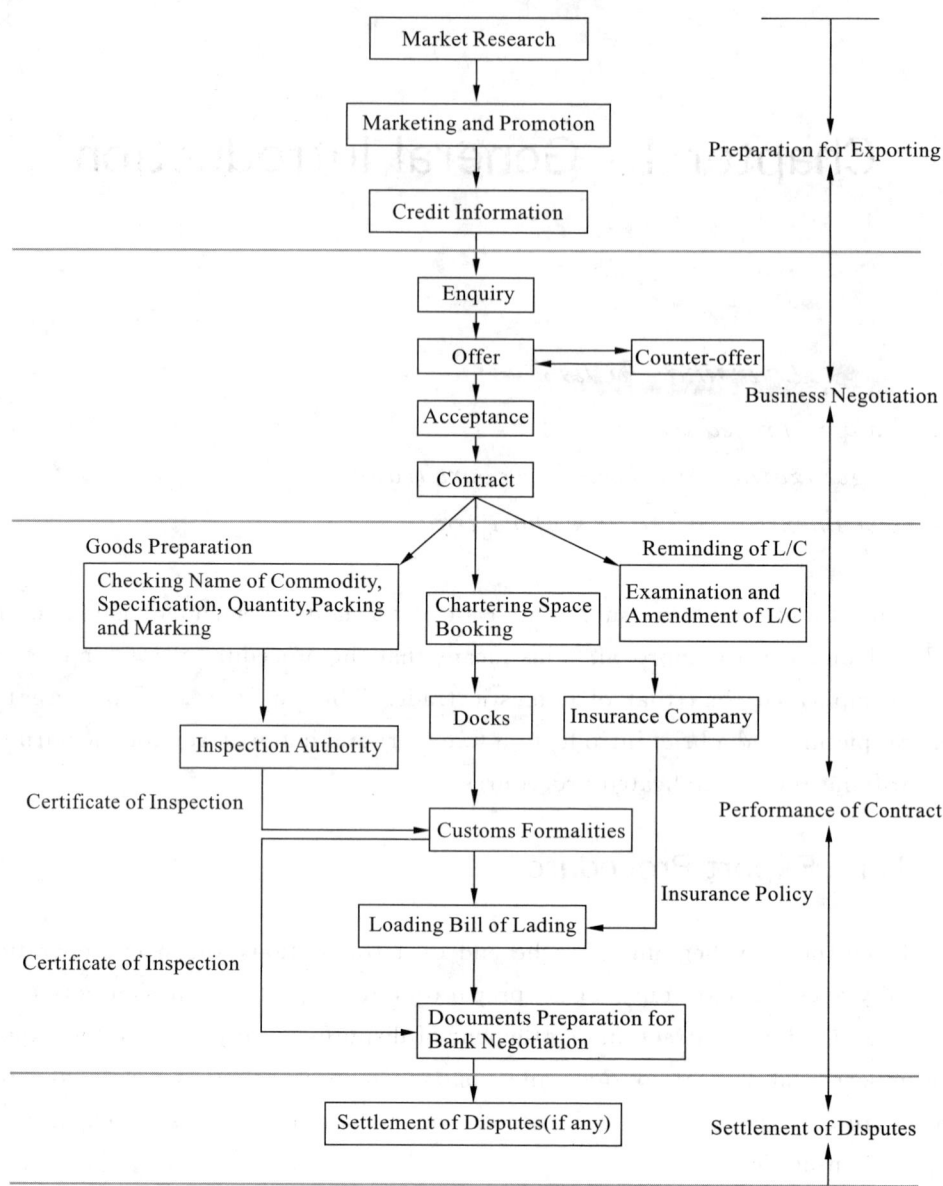

Export procedure under L/C and CIF

foreign trade, foreign exchange control, customs tariffs and commercial practices. A research should also be conducted about the production, consumption, price and its trend. Besides, the exporter should know what kind of reputation the importer has, the size of his business, how he pays his accounts as customers with good credit standing will facilitate the export trade.

In addition to conducting research, the exporter can also take the initiative to promote his products in the overseas market through the frequently adopted strategies.

1.1.2 Business negotiation

Generally speaking, negotiation consists of the following steps: inquiry, offer, counter-offer, acceptance and conclusion of sales contract. Offer and acceptance are two indispensable steps for reaching an agreement and concluding a contract.

Inquiry   An inquiry is a request for business information, such as price lists, samples and details about the goods or trade terms. It is usually made by the importer.

Offer   On receiving the inquiry, exporter should reply to it without delay to start the business. An offer is a proposal made by the sellers to buyers to enter into a contract.

Counter-offer   A reply to an offer which purports to be an acceptance but contains additions, limitations is a rejection of the offer and constitutes a counter-offer.

Acceptance   Acceptance is a statement made by the offeree indicating unconditional assent to an offer. A contract is concluded once the acceptance is effective.

1.1.3 Implementation of contract

Under the CIF contract with terms of payment by L/C, the implementation of contract usually goes through several steps.

Reminding, examining and amending L/C   After signing the sales contract, the seller should urge the buyer to establish L/C through his bank as sometimes the L/C is delayed for various reasons. Upon receipt of a letter of credit, the seller must examine it carefully to ensure that all terms and conditions are in accordance with the contract. If there is any discrepancy, the seller should contact the buyer for necessary amendments.

Preparing goods for shipment   The main task for the seller is to prepare the goods for shipment and check them against terms stipulated in the contract.

Inspection formalities If required by the stipulations of the contract, the seller should obtain a certificate of inspection from the institutions concerned where the goods are inspected.

Chartering and booking shipping space After receiving the relevant L/C, the seller should contact the shipping agents for the chartering and booking shipping space, and prepare for the shipment in accordance with the contract.

Insurance Under CIF term, the seller should insure the goods sold for export against the perils of the journey. The cover paid for will vary according to the type of goods and the circumstance.

Customs declaration Before the goods are loaded, customs formalities have to be completed. Certain documents such as the copy of contract, invoice, packing list, weight memo, inspection certificate, shipping order and other relevant documents have to be lodged with the customs.

Loading and transportation After going through the customs formalities, the goods can be loaded on board the vessel at the named port of shipment. The shipping company or the ship's agent will issue a bill of lading which is a receipt evidencing the loading of the goods on board the ship.

Documents preparation for negotiation After the shipment, all kinds of documents required by the L/C should be prepared by the exporter and presented within the time limit of the L/C to the bank for negotiation. Documents should be correct and complete. Only after the documents are checked to be fully in accordance with the L/C, the bank makes payment.

1.1.4 Settlement of disputes

Claims are likely to be caused by various reasons such as more or less quantity delivered, poor packaging, inferior quality, discrepancy between the samples and the goods, delay in shipment, etc. Once disputes arise, arbitration is better than litigation, and friendly negotiation is better than arbitration.

1.2 Organizations Involved in Export Trade

All or most of the following organizations are involved in an export and import transaction:

Chapter 1 General Introduction

Exporter
Chamber of commerce(in some cases)
Shipping agent
Port authority
Shipping company
Insurance company
Exporter's bank
Importer's bank
Customs
Inspection authority
Arbitration commission (in some cases)
Importer

1.3 Documents Involved in Export Trade

An export and import transaction usually requires a lot of complicated documents. The number and types of documents needed depend on the specific requirements of the exporter and the importer. Generally, the documents needed include:

Commercial invoice
Proforma invoice
Packing list
Weight memo
Certificate of inspection
Certificate of origin
Insurance policy
Bill of lading
Sales contract

Chapter 2 Preparation

Establishing trade relations

2.1 Market Research and Promotion

Before planning to sell the products in a foreign country, any exporter must carry out a lot of researches. He must answer such questions as: Is there a good demand for the products in the new market? Are they allowed to be imported? If so, what is the import duty? What is the market price and its trend at that end? Is the landed price competitive compared with other competitive products? What about the economic, financial and political stability of the importing country? What about the local laws and regulations governing foreign trade, customs tariffs, and commercial practices?

The exporter can get the desired information about foreign market from many sources like government departments concerned, customs offices, trade associations, private business firms, trade journals, advertising media, banks and other business people, etc.

After studying the information through market research, the exporter may decide and take measures to promote the goods to that market. Promotion is an indispensable part of the Marketing Mix. There are several ways in promotion:

Sales literature   Brochures, catalogues and leaflets can describe your products in more details.

Sponsorship   You can contribute to the cost of a sporting or artistic event, where the brand name of your product can be displayed prominently.

Public relations   Public relations can guarantee that you keep a high profile.

Packaging Labels increase the impact of your product.

Exhibitions Customers can see a display or a demonstration of your products and get hands-on experience.

Point of sale advertising Displays in retail outlets can attract the attention of potential customers.

2.2　Establishing Trade Relations

There are some ways to get information of prospective clients:
- Trade Directory/Union 贸易名录/行会
- Chamber of Commerce both at home and abroad 国内外商会
  China Chamber of International Commerce (CCOIC) 中国国际商会
- Embassies or consulates/The commercial counselor's office of the embassy in foreign countries　大使馆驻国外商务参赞处
- Advertisements in the newspaper or periodicals
- Banks
- Market survey/research 市场调研
- Mutual visits by trade delegations and representatives 贸易代表互访
- Introduction from other business firms or friends or business house of the same trade 同业商行
- The Internet
- Market investigation
- Attendance at the export commodities fairs and exhibitions at home and abroad 出口商品展会

After knowing the information about your client, you may begin to write letters or e-mails to establish business relations. Here are two sample letters of establishing business relations.

Sample Letter One:

本公司于1952年成立,专营玩具和工艺品,现在已经成为中国最大的进出口公司之一。由于公司的产品质量高、价格优惠,因此在世界各地的客户中享有较高声誉。2014年3月你从国际互联网络上得知美国的 DRAGON TOY CO.,LTD 欲求购中国产的遥控赛车(Telecontrol Racing Car)。客户的详细地址如下:

DRAGON TOY CO.,LTD

1180 CHURCH ROAD NEW YORK,

PA 19446 USA.

FAX：215-393-3921

E-MAIL ADDRESS：timzsh0516@sina.com

请参照上述基本情况，根据草拟建立业务关系信函的基本要求给对方发一封建立业务关系的电子邮件，要求格式完整、正确，内容包括公司介绍、产品介绍，并另寄产品目录及表达想与对方建交的热切愿望等。

Date：Dec. 26th, 2014

DRAGON TOY CO. ,LTD

1180 CHURCH ROAD NEW YORK,

PA 19446 USA

FAX：215-393-3921

E-MAIL ADDRESS：timzsh0516@sina.com

Dear Sir or Madam,

We obtained your name and address from the international internet in March 2014 and we know that you are interested in Telecontrol Racing Car produced in China. Now we are writing to you to hope to establish business relations with you.

Our company was founded in 1952, specializing in toy and handicraft, and has already become one of the biggest import & export companies in China now. Our products hold high reputation by the clients in the world with the high quality and favorable price. Telecontrol Racing Car is our new product and it is very popular all over the world.

In order to give you a general idea of various kinds of product that we are handling, we are airmailing you under separate cover our latest catalogue for your reference. Please let us know immediately if you are interested in our products.

We look forward to your early reply.

Yours faithfully,

Jerry

Chapter 2 Preparation

Sample Letter Two:

我方在 2014 年 10 月 23 日举办的广交会上得知美国 TCP 公司需要节能灯。美国 TCP 公司（TCP COMPANY, USA）成立于 1986 年, 是一家跨国大型光源公司, 主要经营各种优质节能灯、节能灯具、电感、电子日光灯用镇流器和灯具, 以及应急安全灯和灯具等。

Dear Sirs,

We have learned from the Canton Fair in October 23, 2014 that you are in the market for energy-saving light.

As a leader in energy-saving lamp industry, we are glad to offer our own services. And we would like to enter into business relations with you on the basis of equality, mutual benefit and the exchange of needed goods.

Our energy-saving lamps are made of fine materials with advanced technology and using traditional craft. The company has passed the CCC certification and ISO9000 certification, so quality is guaranteed. Our lamps are your first choice because of the reasonable price. We ensure a catalogue for your reference and would have a keen on receiving your inquiries.

We look forward to your early reply.

Yours faithfully,
Jerry

Useful expressions:

(1) Source of information

We owe your name and address to...

We obtain your name and address from...

Through the courtesy of..., we come to know your name and address.

You were recommended to our company by...

Having had your name and address from...

We learned from... that you are producing shoes and handbags for export.

(2) Brief introduction of your own company

We would like to introduce ourselves to you as a corporation specializing in the export business of electric and electronic equipment.

We would like to offer you our services as a trading firm, and would mention that we have excellent connections in the trade and are fully experienced in the import business for this kind of product.

Our corporation specializes in the export of textiles.

Our company was listed on the New York Stock Exchange in 1999.

We are a Sino-US joint venture with a registered capital of USD 20 million.

We are one of the largest importers of building materials in the Southeast Asian.

(3) The intention of writing the letter

We are interested in establishing business relations with your corporation for the purpose of supplying you the commodities you want.

We would like to offer you our services as a trading firm, and...

We are writing to you in the hope that we can open up business relations with your firm.

In order to extend our export business to your country, we wish to enter into direct business relations with you.

We wish to express our desire to trade with you in leather shoes.

(4) Provide or ask for catalogue, price list and samples

To give you a general idea of our products, we are sending you under separate cover our latest catalogue together with a range of pamphlets for your reference.

We are enclosing a catalogue and a pricelist for your reference, so that you may acquaint yourselves with some of the items we handle.

In order to give you a general idea of our canned goods, we are sending you by separate airmail a copy of our latest catalogue. Quotations and samples will be sent to you upon receipt of your specific inquiries.

We invite you to send us details and prices, possibly samples.

In order to let us have a better understanding of your products, would you please send us catalogues and prices of your products with full details. Upon receipt of such materials, we shall see what items are of interest to us and pass our inquiries to you.

(5) Provide reference about financial standing or credit

If you need more objective information concerning our credit, please refer to the Midland Bank, London.

Concerning our financial status and reputation, please direct all inquiries to Bank of China, Beijing in China.

(6) Polite ending (expect to get the reply)

We look forward to hearing from you soon.

We look forward to your early/favorable reply.

We expect your prompt reply.

Your early reply will be appreciated.

We look forward to your order.

Please contact us at your earliest convenience.

We look forward to the opportunity of doing business with you.

Exercise

I. Translate the following terms and expressions

A. Into Chinese:
1. look forward to
2. a favorable reply
3. establishment of trade relations
4. full details
5. items available for export now
6. import and export now
7. circular letter
8. specific price
9. favorable price
10. enclosed please find

B. Into English:
1. 建立贸易关系
2. 潜在的买主/客户
3. 棉布
4. 经营范围
5. 早日
6. 概况
7. 种类繁多的
8. 价格单
9. 样品本
10. 收到……后

II. Choose the best answer to complete each of the following sentences

1. ____ in 1995, this company specializes in the export of cotton piece goods.
   A. Establish   B. Established   C. Establishing   D. To be established
2. ____ please find the catalogues and latest price list.
   A. Enclosed   B. Enclosing   C. Enclose   D. Enclosure
3. We will forward all the necessary information of the item mentioned above ____ receipt of your reply.
   A. with   B. upon   C. in   D. of

4. We look forward ____ your favorable news.
   A. on   B. to   C. at   D. of
5. The present market is favorable ____ importers.
   A. with   B. for   C. in   D. to
6. Because the article falls ____ the scope of our business activities, we are writing you in hope of ____ trade relations with you.
   A. within, establishment   B. within, establishing
   C. below, set up   D. below, setting up
7. Thank you for the sample cutting ____ in your letter.
   A. enclose   B. enclosed   C. enclosing   D. being enclosed
8. We take the pleasure of introducing ourselves ____ an experienced importer ____ line of daily products.
   A. of, on   B. as, in   C. for, by   D. be, at
9. Thank you for your price list showing various kinds of products now ____ for export.
   A. available   B. be available   C. to be available   D. being available
10. ____ create severe competition for home produced goods.
    A. Import   B. Importing   C. Imports   D. Imported

Ⅲ. Translate the following sentences into Chinese

1. We are willing to enter into business relations with your company(公司) on the basis of equality and mutual benefits.
2. We write to introduce ourselves as one of the leading exporters of a wide range of air conditioners(空调).
3. In order to export our products to Western Europe, we are writing to you to seek cooperation possibilities(合作机会).
4. We have a lot of colors and sizes to meet different needs.
5. We have airmailed you some leaflets about our products. If you are interested in any of the items, please let us know.
6. With years of efforts, we have enlarged our business scope and now we deal in nearly 100 kinds of goods.
7. Our main business covers the import and export of various light industrial products.

8. If your corporation does not import the goods mentioned above, please give this letter to a firm who may be concerned.
9. As an exporter of motor bicycle, we wish to express our desire to trade with you in this line.
10. To give a general idea of products, we are sending you separately a catalogue together with three pamphlets for your information.

Ⅳ. *Translate the following sentences into English*
1. 兹介绍,本公司是一家人造珠宝(imitation jewelry)的出口公司,在这一行已有多年经验。
2. 你上周写给总部(the headquarter)的信已转交给我们公司,因该产品属我们经营。
3. 我们可供出口的轻工产品(light industrial products)种类繁多。
4. 很高兴收到你方内附插图目录的来信。
5. 我们盼望收到你们对于我们产品的具体要求。
6. 我们是一家信誉良好的私人公司(private company),非常希望与你们建立贸易关系。
7. 经理简单地给我介绍了一下Johnson公司的情况,他们有可能成为我们的客户。
8. 为了让你们对表格中的产品有个大体了解,特随附小册子及最新的价格单各一份。
9. 当出口值超过进口值,被称为贸易顺差。
10. 我们的产品质量(quality)上乘,价格优惠。

Ⅴ. *Translate the following letter into English*
先生:
　　我们从上周的《中国日报》获悉,贵方对丝绸服装感兴趣。兹介绍本公司,是我地服装行业最大的出口商。我们愿意与你方在平等互利的基础上建立贸易关系。
　　我们的真丝服装采用高档真丝面料,由传统工艺加工而成。现随附一份插图目录及最新价格单供你方参考。如有意,请寄具体询价。收到后,当即航寄报价及样品。
　　盼早复。

商祺

Ⅵ. *Write an English letter in a proper form based on the following information*

Write a letter to Foothill Enterprises Trade Development Co., Ltd (P. O. Box 22789 Taiz Street, Sana'a, Republic of Yemen) telling them:

1. You are introduced by the Commercial Counselor's Office of their embassy in Beijing(驻北京的大使馆商务参赞处).
2. You wish to set up business relations with them.
3. The main scope of your business is exporting chinaware(瓷器).
4. Samples and catalogues will be sent to them upon receipt of their specific inquiries.

Chapter 3 Business Negotiation

Inquiry
Offer
Counter-offer
Acceptance
Sales contract

3.1 Inquiry

3.1.1 What is inquiry?

When a businessman wants to import, he may send out an inquiry to an exporter, inviting a quotation or an offer for the goods he wishes to buy or simply asking for some general information about these goods. Business negotiations usually begin with an inquiry by an overseas buyer to seller, inquiring about the terms and conditions of a sale. According to the content or purpose, an inquiry may be either a general inquiry or a specific inquiry.

3.1.2 What should a letter of inquiry cover?

Model letter of inquiry:

> Dear sirs
>
> We have heard from British Embassy in Paris that you are producing for export hand-made shoes and gloves in natural materials.

> There is a steady demand in France for high-quality goods of this type. Sales are not high, but a good price can be obtained for fashionable designs.
>
> Will you please send us your catalogue and full details of your export prices and terms of payment, together with samples of leathers used in your articles and, if possible, specimens of some of the articles themselves?
>
> We are looking forward to hearing from you.
>
> Sincerely yours,
>
> Jerry

A first inquiry should include:

A brief mention of how you obtained your potential supplier's name.

Indication of the demand in your area for the goods which the supplier deals in.

Details of what you would like your prospective supplier to send you.

A closing sentence.

3.2 Offer

3.2.1 Definition

According to *the United Nations Convention on Contracts for the International Sale of Goods*[①], a proposal for concluding a contract addressed to one or more specific persons constitutes an offer if it is sufficiently definite and indicates the intention of the offeror to be bound in case of acceptance. A mere introduction of goods is not an offer and can not be accepted to form a valid contract. In other words, an offer is actually a proposal of certain trade terms and an expression of a willingness to make a contract according to the terms proposed. These terms mainly include name of commodity, quantity, price, specification,

---

①*United Nations Convention on Contracts for Sale of Goods*(CISG)(《联合国国际货物销售契约公约》) is an international trade agreement. The CISG applies to contracts between companies located in different countries. Over two-thirds of the world's countries have adopted this agreement.

packing, shipment and payment, etc.

3.2.2 Basic conditions

An effective offer should follow four basic conditions:

(1) An offer should be addressed to one or more specific persons.

(2) An offer should be sufficiently definite.

(3) An offer should indicate the intention of the offerer to be bound in case of acceptance.

(4) An offer should reach the offeree. It is effective upon reaching the offeree.

Question: Can we consider commercial advertisements and price lists as an offer?

3.2.3 Withdrawal and revocation

Withdrawal: An offer may be withdrawn if the withdrawal reaches the offeree before or at the same time as the offer.

Revocation: An offer may be revoked if the revocation reaches the offeree before he has dispatched an acceptance.

Question: Which happens before an offer becomes effective, withdrawal or revocation?

Case study:

A 在 2 月 17 日上午用航空信寄出一份实盘给 B，A 在发盘通知中注有"不可撤销"(Irrevocable)的字样，规定受盘人 B 在 2 月 25 日前答复有效。但 A 又于 2 月 17 日下午用电报发出撤回通知(Notice of withdrawal)，该通知于 2 月 18 日上午送达 B 处。B 于 2 月 19 日才收到 A 空邮来的实盘，由于 B 考虑到发盘的价格对他十分有利，于是立即用电报发出接受通知。事后双方对合同是否成立问题发生纠纷。问 A 与 B 之间合同是否成立？为什么？

3.2.4 Termination

An offer can be terminated in the following cases:

(1) Counter-offer terminates an offer.

(2) An offer may lapse if it is beyond the time limit.

(3) An offer may come to an end if the offerer revokes the offer.

(4) Force majeure terminates an offer.

(5) Offer may lapse when one party is dead, becomes incompetent or goes bankrupt.

3.2.5 Firm offer and non-firm offer

An offer can either be a firm offer or a non-firm offer.

A firm offer is a kind of offer which is made to a specific person or persons to express or imply a definite intention of the offerer to make a contract under a clear, complete and final trade terms. It specifies a time limit for which the offer is valid. Once it is unconditionally accepted by the offeree within its time limit, this firm offer can not be revoked or amended and is binding upon both parties.

Unlike a firm offer, a non-firm offer is an offer without engagement. It is unclear, incomplete and with reservation. It has no binding force upon the offerer. Moreover, the offerer makes the offer with reservation: this offer is subject to his final confirmation; this offer is for your reference only.

The differences between a firm offer and a non-firm offer is that: in making a firm offer, the exporter cannot take the offer back, and it usually has the time limit. On the other hand, the exporter can take back a non-firm offer at will.

An example of firm offer and non-firm offer:

Dear sirs,

We thank you for your letter of July 10, 1998 and have pleasure in offering you the following:

Commodity: embroidered mini skirts

Quantity: 10 000 dozens

Price: $50 per dozen CFR New York

Packing: in see-through plastic bags

Shipment: in August 1998

Payment: by irrevocable L/C, payable by draft at sight

This offer is subject to our confirmation. Should you require any further information about our products, please do not hesitate to contact us.

Yours sincerely,
Jerry

3.2.6 A letter of offer

A letter of offer should include:
(1) Express thanks for inquiry
(2) Name of commodity, quality, quantity and specification
(3) Details of price, discounts and terms of payment
(4) Packing and delivery time
(5) The period for which the offer is valid
(6) Closing sentence

Case study:
中国国家工艺品进出口有限公司收到苏丹贸易有限公司 5 月 12 日的询问关于货号为 No.512 款瓷器的询价信。现报虚盘如下:No.512:USD 50 per dozen CIF C 5% Port Sudan,数量为 3400 dozens,支付方式为保兑不可撤销信用证,要求立即装运,并根据对方要求另寄样品。

Suggested answer:

Dear sirs,

In reply to your letter of/dated April 12 concerning/regarding the chinaware, we are giving an offer, subject to our final confirmation as follows:

Commodity: chinaware
Article No.: 512
Price: USD 50 per dozen CIF C 5% Port Sudan
Quantity: 3400 dozens
Shipment: prompt shipment

Payment: confirmed, irrevocable letter of credit

Under separate cover, we are sending you samples required.

It is known to all that the Chinese chinaware is exquisitely made and moderately priced. It is hoped that you will send us your orders as early as possible.

Yours sincerely,
Jerry

3.3　Counter-offer

If the offeree deems the price in the offer is on the high side, some terms and conditions do not agree to what he expected, he may reject the offer, or most probably, make a counter-offer.

A reply to an offer which purports to be an acceptance but contains additions, limitations or other modifications is a rejection of the offer and constitutes a counter-offer. Therefore, a counter-offer is, in fact, a new offer, at the same time, the original offer lapses.

A letter of counter-offer should include:

Thank the seller for his offer

Express regret at inability to accept

Make a counter-offer

Suggest other opportunities later

Case study:

我国某外贸企业向国外询购某商品,不久接到外商3月20日的发盘,有效期至3月26日。我方于3月22日电复:"如能把单价降低5美元,可以接受。"对方没有反应。后因用货部门要货心切,又鉴于该商品行市看涨,我方随即于3月25日去电表示同意对方3月20日发盘所提的条件。试分析:此项交易是否达成? 理由何在?

3.4 Acceptance

An acceptance is a statement made by the offeree indicating assent to an offer. Acceptance validates the contract. In other words, once the acceptance becomes effective, the sales contract comes into effect.

3.4.1 Requirements for an acceptance

(1) An acceptance must be made by the specific offeree.

(2) An acceptance must be made by offeree and received by the offerer within the valid period of a firm offer.

(3) An acceptance must materially agree with the offer. A reply to an offer which purports to be an acceptance but contains additions, limitations or other modifications is a rejection of the offer and constitutes a counter-offer. However, a reply to an offer which purports to be an acceptance but contains additional or different terms which do not materially alter the terms of the offer constitutes an acceptance, unless the offerer, without undue delay, objects orally to the discrepancy or dispatches a written notice to that effect.

公约认为的实质性条件:货物的价格,付款条件,交货的时间、地点,货物的质量、数量,当事人的赔偿责任范围,解决争议的方法等。

e.g. 某公司对外发盘,国外客户收到发盘后在有效期内做出回复表示接受,但同时又指出:如果双方发生争议,应提交仲裁委员会进行仲裁。问:该项接受是否有效?

(4) An acceptance must be clearly expressed by the offeree's verbal or written statement. Acceptance can also be made by performing an act. Silence or inactivity is by no means an acceptance.

3.4.2 Late acceptance

An acceptance beyond the time limit of offer would be a late acceptance and then it is up to the offerer to inform the offeree if the offerer wants to take the late acceptance as an effective acceptance. The following is the article of the convention:

(1) A late acceptance is nevertheless effective as an acceptance if without delay the offeror orally informs the offeree or dispatches a notice to that effect.

(2) If a letter or other writing containing a late acceptance shows that has been sent in such circumstances that if its transmission had been normal it would have reached the offeror in due time, the late acceptance is effective as an acceptance unless, without delay, the offeror orally informs the offeree that he considers his offer as having lapsed or dispatches a notice to that effect.

3.4.3 Withdrawal

According to the convention, an acceptance becomes effective when it is received by the offerer and a contract is concluded at the moment when an acceptance of an offer becomes effective. An acceptance can be withdrawn if the withdrawal reaches the offerer before or at the same time with the acceptance. However, an acceptance can not be revoked.

3.5 Contract

Words concerning contract:
Nouns:
cancellation/breach of/violation 取消、破坏、违反
completion/execution/performance 完成、履行
expiration/renewal 到期、续订
verbs:
abide by 遵守
alter, amend 修改
annul 废除, annulment/cancel 取消
execute/implement/carry out, perform, fulfill 执行/draft, draw up 起草
enforce 强制执行
enter into 缔结
extend 延长
terminate 解除
to bring a contract into effect 使合同生效
to come into effect 生效
to cease to be in effect/force 失效
to tear up the contract 撕毁合同
to approve the contract 审批合同

to be legally binding 受法律约束
to secure one's agreement 征得……的同意
contract price 合约价格
contract wages 合同工资
contract note 买卖合同(证书)
contract of employment 雇佣合同
contract of engagement 雇佣合同
contract of carriage 运输合同
contract of arbitration 仲裁合同
contract for goods 订货合同
contract for purchase 采购合同
contract for service 劳务合同
contract for future delivery 期货合同
contract of sale 销售合同
contract of insurance 保险合同
to ship a contract 装运货物的合同
contractual dispute 合同的争议
a long-term contract 长期合同
a short-term contract 短期合同
contract parties 合同当事人
contractual practice 合同惯例
contractual claim 根据合同的债权
contractual liability/obligation 合同规定的义务
contractual specifications 合同规定
contractual terms & conditions 合同条款和条件
contractual guarantee 合同规定的担保
contractual damage 合同引起的损害
contractual-joint-venture 合作经营,契约式联合经营
completion of contract 完成合同
interpretation of contract 解释合同
originals of the contract 合同原件
copies of the contract 合同副本

3.5.1　Two samples of sales contract

Sample one:

CONTRACT

No.:_____
Date:_____
Seller:_____
Address:_____
Buyer:_____
Address:_____

This contract is made by and between the buyer and the seller, whereby the buyer agrees to buy and the seller agrees to sell the under-mentioned commodity according to the terms and conditions stipulated below:

(1) Name of commodities

(2) Specification: moisture(max.) 15%, admixture(max.)2%

(3) Packing terms: to be packed in new gunny bags of 50kg net each

(4) Quantities: 118Mt

(5) Unit price: USD226/Mt CFR Pusan

(6) Total value: USD 26,668.00, with 5% more or less both in amount and quantity allowed at the seller's option

(7) Shipping Marks

(8) Time of Shipping: by 15 Oct,1999

(9) Loading Port & Destination: from Tianjin to Pusan, partial shipments allowed

(10) Insurance: to be effected by the buyer

(11) Terms of Payment

By confirmed, irrevocable, transferable and banker's acceptance L/C at sight with partial shipment, remaining valid for negotiation in China until 15th day after the time of shipment. The L/C shall be opened within 3 days after the signing of the contract. The L/C shall be opened in favor of the seller.

(12) Documents

The seller shall present the following documents to the negotiating bank:

(a) Full set of clean on board ocean Bills of Lading made out to ____/to order of ____ and bank endorsed marked "Freight Prepaid/to Collect";

(b) Commercial Invoice _____;
(c) Under the term of CIF, Insurance Policy/Insurance Certificate;
(d) Packing List _____;
(e) Quality Certificate;
(f) Certificate of Origin.

(13) Terms of Shipment

The carrying vessel shall be provided by the sellers. Partial shipments and transshipment are allowed.

After loading is completed, the seller shall notify the buyer by cable of the contract number, name of commodity, quantity, name of the carrying vessel and date of shipment.

(14) Quality/Quantity Discrepancy and Claim

In case the quality and/or quantity/weight of the goods found by the buyer are not in conformity with the provisions of the contract after arrival of the goods at the port of destination, the buyer may lodge claim with the seller on such strength of the inspection certificate issued by an inspection organization as is agreed by the parties to the contract, with the exception, however, of the claims for which the insurance company and/or the shipping company are to be held responsible. Claim for quality discrepancy shall, within 30 days after arrival of the goods at the port of destination, be filed by the buyer. While for quantity/weight discrepancy claims shall, within 15 days after arrival of the goods at the port of destination, be filed by the buyer. The seller shall, within 30 days after receipt of the claim requirement, reply to the buyer.

(15) Force Majeure

The Seller shall not be held responsible for failure or delay to perform all or any part of its obligations specified in the contract due to flood, fire, earthquake, drought, war or any other events which could not be predicted at the time of the conclusion of the contract, and could not be controlled, avoided or overcome by the seller. Provided that the seller shall, as soon as possible, inform the other party of its occurrence in written form and thereafter send a certificate of the event issued by the relevant authority to the other party thereto within 15 days after its occurrence. If the force majeure event last over 20 days, the parties thereto shall negotiate the execution or the termination of the Contract.

(16) Arbitration

All disputes in connection with this contract or the execution thereof shall be settled by negotiation between two parties. If no settlement can be reached, the case in dispute shall then be submitted for arbitration in the country of defendant in accordance with the arbitration regulations of the arbitration organization of the defendant country. The decision made by the arbitration organization shall be taken as final and binding upon both parties. The arbitration expenses shall be borne by the losing party unless otherwise awarded by the arbitration organization.

(17) Remarks

The seller: _____

The buyer: _____

Sample two:

CONTRACT

No:

Date:

For Account of:

Indent No:

This contract is made by and between the sellers and the buyers; Whereby the sellers agree to sell and the buyers agree to buy the undermentioned goods according to the terms and conditions stipulated below and overleaf:

(1) Names of commodity (ies) and specification(s):

(2) Quantity:

(3) Unit price:

(4) Amount TOTAL: _____% more or less allowed

(5) Packing:

(6) Port of Loading:

(7) Port of Destination:

(8) Shipping Marks:

(9) Time of Shipment: Within _____ days after receipt of L/C, allowing transshipment and partial shipment.

(10) Terms of Payment: By 100% Confirmed, Irrevocable and Sight Letter of Credit to remain valid for negotiation in China until the 15th day after shipment.

Chapter 3 Business Negotiation

(11) Insurance: Covers all risks and war risks only for 110% of the invoice value by ____.

(12) Terms of payment: The Buyer shall, ____ days after this Contract comes into effect, open an irrevocable Letter of Credit in favor of the Seller. The Letter of Credit shall expire ____ days after the completion of loading of the shipment.

(13) Documents: The Sellers shall present to the negotiating bank Clean on Board Bill of Lading, Invoice, Quality Certificate issued by the China Commodity Inspection Bureau or the Manufacturers, Survey Report on Quantity/Weight issued by the China Commodity Inspection Bureau, and Transferable Insurance policy or Insurance Certificate when this contract is made on CIF basis.

(14) Quality/Quantity Discrepancy: In case of quality discrepancy, claim should be filed by the Buyer within 30 days after the arrival of the goods at port of destination. While for quantity discrepancy, claim should be filed by the Buyer within 15 days after the arrival of the goods at port of destination. It is understood that the Seller shall not be liable for any discrepancy of the goods shipped due to causes for which the Insurance Company, Shipping Company, other transportation organizations and/or Post Office are liable.

(15) Force Majeure: The Seller shall not be held liable for failure or delay in delivery of the entire lot or a portion of the goods under this Sales Contract due to any Force Majeure incidents. (Force majure, such as heavy weather, lightning, tsunami, flood, earth quake, fire, explosion, collision and uncontrollable events.)

(16) Arbitration: All disputes in connection with this contract or the execution thereof shall be settled friendly through negotiations. In case no settlement can be reached, the case may then be submitted for arbitration to China International Economic and Trade Arbitration Commission in accordance with the provisional Rules of Procedures promulgated by the Arbitration Commission. The decision of the Arbitration Commission shall be final and binding upon both parties, neither party shall seek recourse to a law court nor other authorities to appeal for revision of the decision. Arbitration fee shall be borne by the losing party. Or arbitration may be settled in the third country mutually agreed upon by both parties.

(17) Other Conditions: This Contract is executed in two counterparts each in Chinese and English, each of which shall be deemed equally authentic. This

Contract is in two copies, effective since being signed by both parties.

Seller: Buyer:

3.5.2 Language features of sales contract

3.5.2.1 Lexical features

(1) Formal words

e.g. "生效期"指的是双方合同签字的日子。

The term "effective date" means the date on which the contract is executed by the parties.

execute＞sign

本合同受中国法律管辖,并按中国法律解释。

This contract shall be governed by and construed in accordance with the laws of China.

construe＞explain, interpret

如一方想出售或转让其投资之全部,另一方有优先购买权。

In case one party desires to sell or assign all its investment subscribed, the other party shall have the preemptive right.

assign＞transfer

Others:

give＜render

help＜assist

stop＜terminate

before＜prior to

begin＜commence

make sure＜confirm

about＜concerning, with regard to

in fact＜in effect

around＜approximately

due to＜by virtue of

consider＜deem

(2) Old English words

here+介词:

    hereunder=under this 本合约内

    hereby=by this 特此

    hereto=to this 关于这个

    hereof=of this 本合同

    herein=in this 在此,在这里

hereinafter 以下

e. g. This contract is entered into and made duplicate by and between A Company (hereinafter referred to as "Party A") and B Company (hereinafter referred to as "Party B").

本销售合同由 ABC 有限公司(以下简称甲方)和 EFG 有限公司(以下简称乙方)于 2009 年 9 月 16 日在中华人民共和国厦门市订立,一式两份。

This sales contract is entered into and made duplicate on 16th of September, 2009 in Xiamen, the People's Republic of China, by and between ABC Co., Ltd. (hereinafter called "Party A" and EFG Co., Ltd. (hereinafter called "Party B").

"hereinafter called/hereinafter referred to as..."表示"以下简称"。

there+介词

    therein=in that

    thereof=of that

    thereto=to that

    thereon=on that

    therefrom=from that

    therefor(e)=for that

    thereafter=after that 此后

where+介词

    whereby=by which

    aforesaid 上述的

    undermentioned 以下的

(3) Use of "shall"

"Shall"在法律英语中有特殊的含义,是一个极为严谨的法律用词,通常表示

法律行为人应享有某种权利和须承担某种义务,但如果与权利、义务无关,则应避免使用。在译文里,通常表示"必须""应当",或"将""可以",有时也不译出来。

e.g. Any dispute between two or more contracting parties concerning the interpretation or application of the Convention which cannot be settled through negotiation, shall, at the request of one of them, be submitted to arbitration.

两个或两个以上的缔约方对本公约的解释或适用发生的争议未能解决时,应根据其中一方的请求提交仲裁。

(此例中的"shall"被译为"应当")

The quality and prices of the commodities to be exchanged between the importers and exporters in the two countries shall be acceptable to both sides and the prices shall be fixed in accordance with world market prices.

货物的质量和价格必须使进出口双方都能接受,而价格必须和国际市场价格一致。

(此例中的"shall"被译为"必须")

The formation of this contract, its validity, interpretation, execution and settlement of the disputes shall be governed by related Laws of the People's Republic of China.

本合同的订立、效力、解释、履行和争议的解决均受中华人民共和国法律的管辖。

(此例中的"shall"不译出来)

通过以上例句不难发现,shall 一词在合同英语中仅表示合同当事人所享有的权利和应履行的义务,尤其是后者,更强调强制履行的性质。因此,在没有表示强制的情况下或与表示权利、义务无关的情况下,不宜使用 shall。

(4) Capitalization

The Buyers, the Sellers, China Council for the Promotion of International Trade, this Contract, China Commodity Inspection Bereau...

(5) Preposition+noun+preposition

  in conflict with
  in accordance with
  in conformity with
  in connection with

e.g. All disputes in connection with this Contract or the execution thereof shall be settled by negotiation between two parties. If no settlement can be reached, the case in dispute shall then be submitted for arbitration in the country of defendant in accordance with the arbitration regulations of the arbitration organization of the defendant country. The decision made by the arbitration organization shall be taken as final and binding upon both parties. The arbitration expenses shall be borne by the losing party unless otherwise awarded by the arbitration organization.

(6) Parallel structures
   final and binding
   terms and conditions
   null and void

本合同有效期从合同生效之日算起共10年,有效期满后,本合同自动失效。

The contract shall be valid for 10 years from the effective date of the contract. On the expiry of the validity term of contract, the contract shall automatically become null and void.

此外还有 made and entered into 和 by and between.

(7) Use of nominalization

(a) If the contracting parties dispute with each other, they shall settle the disputes through...

(b) Should there be any disputes between the contracting parties, they shall be settled through...

(a) The both parties that fulfilled the contract satisfactorily will be the basis for the development of business and further co-operation.

(b) The satisfactory fulfillment of the contract by both parties will be the basis for the development of business and further co-operation. (nominalization)

In this example, the nominalized form fulfillment of the contract is transformed from the clause fulfilled the contract.

(a) The quality, quantity, condition and/or weight of the goods ordered by the buyer shall strictly conform to the contract stipulations.

(b) The quality, quantity, condition and/or weight of the goods ordered by the buyer shall be in strict/exact conformity with the contract stipulations. (nominalization)

以上三组句子中,句子(b)都使用了名物化结构,突出了合同语言的客观性和正式程度。

3.5.2.2 Syntactic features

(1) Conditional clause

商务合同中存在大量的条件句式,而这些条件句通常由以下几个词引导:if, in case of/that, provided that, in the event of/that, unless, should, where+an adverbial clause, whereas+an adverbial clause

unless otherwise+p. p（除非）

e. g. Should any other clause in this contract be in conflict with the supplementary conditions, the supplementary conditions should be taken as final and binding.

本合同其他任何条款如与本附加条款有抵触时,以本附加条款为准。

Whereas you have breached the contract, we have no option but to lodge a claim on you for the losses incurred.

鉴于你方违反了合同,我们不得不就所造成的损失向你方进行索赔。

(2) Prepositional phrase

① This sales contract is entered into and made duplicate *on 16th of September, 2009 in Xiamen, the People's Republic of China*, by and between ABC Co.,Ltd. (hereinafter called "Party A" and EFG Co., Ltd. (hereinafter called "Party B").

② The buyer shall, 15 *days before the date of shipment specified in the contract*, notify the contract number for the seller to effect shipment.

③ ____ as one party and ____ as the other party agree to sign by their authorized representatives, *as a result of friendly negotiation*, the present contract under the following terms and conditions.

④ Claim for quality discrepancy shall, *within 30 days after arrival of the goods at the port of destination*, be filed by the buyer.

3.5.2.3 Textual features

(1) Preamble: the name of each party, residential address; contract No.,

the date and place of signature of contract.

(2) Body.

(3) The tail: language to be used in the contract and their effectiveness.

e. g. This contract is executed in two counterparts each in Chinese and English, each of which shall be deemed equally authentic. This contract is in two copies, effective since being signed by both parties.

The following articles concerning the formation of the contract from *United Nations Convention on Contracts for Sale of Goods* can help us to further understand the requirements for the construction of a contract.

第二部分 合同的订立

PART II   Formation of the Contract

第 14 条

(1)向一个或一个以上特定的人提出的订立合同的建议,如果十分确定并且表明发价人在得到接受时承受约束的意旨,即构成发价。一个建议如果写明货物并且明示或暗示地规定数量和价格或规定如何确定数量和价格,即为十分确定。

(2)非向一个或一个以上特定的人提出的建议,仅应视为邀请做出发价,除非提出建议的人明确地表示相反的意向。

Article 14

(1) A proposal for concluding a contract addressed to one or more specific persons constitutes an offer if it is sufficiently definite and indicates the intention of the offeror to be bound in case of acceptance. A proposal is sufficiently definite if it indicates the goods and expressly or implicitly fixes or makes provision for determining the quantity and the price.

(2) A proposal other than one addressed to one or more specific persons is to be considered merely as an invitation to make offers, unless the contrary is clearly indicated by the person making the proposal.

第 15 条

(1)发价于送达被发价人时生效。

(2)一项发价,即使是不可撤销的,如果撤回通知于发价送达被发价人之前或同时,送达被发价人,可得予撤回。

Article 15

(1) An offer becomes effective when it reaches the offeree.

(2) An offer, even if it is irrevocable, may be withdrawn if the withdrawal reaches the offeree before or at the same time as the offer.

第 16 条

(1)在未订立合同之前,发价得予撤销,如果撤销通知于被发价人发出接受通知之前送达被发价人。

(2)但在下列情况下,发价不得撤销:

(a)发价写明接受发价的期限或以其他方式表示发价是不可撤销的;或

(b)被发价人有理由信赖该项发价是不可撤销的,而且被发价人已本着对该项发价的信赖行事。

Article 16

(1) Until a contract is concluded an offer may be revoked if the revocation reaches the offeree before he has dispatched an acceptance.

(2) However, an offer can not be revoked:

(a) If it indicates, whether by stating a fixed time for acceptance or otherwise, that it is irrevocable; or

(b) If it was reasonable for the offeree to rely on the offer as being irrevocable and the offeree has acted in reliance on the offer.

第 17 条

一项发价,即使是不可撤销的,于拒绝通知送达发价人时终止。

Article 17

An offer, even if it is irrevocable, is terminated when a rejection reaches the offeror.

第 18 条

(1)被发价人声明或做出其他行为表示同意一项发价,即是接受,缄默或不行动本身不等于接受。

(2)接受发价于表示同意的通知送达发价人时生效。如果表示同意的通知在发价人所规定的时间内,如未规定时间,在一段合理的时间内,未曾送达发价人,接受就成为无效,但须适当地考虑到交易的情况,包括发价人所使用的通信方法的迅速程度。对口头发价必须立即接受,但情况有别者不在此限。

(3)但若根据该项发价或依当事人之间确立的习惯作法和惯例,被发价人可以做出某种行为,例如与发运货物或支付价款有关的行为来表示同意,而无须向发价人发出通知,则接受于该项行为做出时生效,但该项行为必须在上一款所规定的期间内做出。

Article 18

(1) A statement made by or other conduct of the offeree indicating assent to an offer is an acceptance. Silence or inactivity does not in itself amount to acceptance.

(2) An acceptance of an offer becomes effective at the moment the indication of assent reaches the offeror. An acceptance is not effective if the indication of assent does not reach the offeror within the time he has fixed or, if no time is fixed, within a reasonable time, due account being taken of the circumstances of the transaction, including the rapidity of the means of communication employed by the offeror. An oral offer must be accepted immediately unless the circumstances indicate otherwise.

(3) However, if, by virtue of the offer or as a result of practices which the parties have established between themselves or of usage, the offeree may indicate assent by performing an act, such as one relating to the dispatch of the goods or payment of the price, without notice to the offeror, the acceptance is effective at the moment the act is performed, provided that the act is performed within the period of time laid down in the preceding paragraph.

第 19 条

(1)对发价表示接受但载有添加、限制或其他更改的答复,即为拒绝该项发价,并构成还价。

(2)但是,对发价表示接受但载有添加或不同条件的答复,如所载的添加或不同条件在实质上并不变更该项发价的条件,除发价人在不过分迟延的期间内以口头或书面通知反对其间的差异外,仍构成接受。如果发价人不做出这种反对,合同的条件就以该项发价的条件以及接受通知内所载的更改为准。

(3)有关货物价格、付款、货物质量和数量、交货地点和时间、一方当事人对另一方当事人的赔偿责任范围或解决争端等的添加或不同条件,均视为在实质上变更发价的条件。

Article 19

(1) A reply to an offer which purports to be an acceptance but contains additions, limitations or other modifications is a rejection of the offer and constitutes a counter-offer.

(2) However, a reply to an offer which purports to be an acceptance but contains additional or different terms which do not materially alter the terms

of the offer constitutes an acceptance, unless the offeror, without undue delay, objects orally to the discrepancy or dispatches a notice to that effect. If he does not so object, the terms of the contract are the terms of the offer with the modifications contained in the acceptance.

(3) Additional or different terms relating, among other things, to the price, payment, quality and quantity of the goods, place and time of delivery, extent of one party's liability to the other or the settlement of disputes are considered to alter the terms of the offer materially.

第 20 条

(1)发价人在电报或信件内规定的接受期间,从电报交发时刻或信上载明的发信日期起算,如信上未载明发信日期,则从信封上所载日期起算。发价人以电话、电传或其他快速通信方法规定的接受期间,从发价送达被发价人时起算。

(2)在计算接受期间时,接受期间内的正式假日或非营业日应计算在内。但是,如果接受通知在接受期间的最后 1 天未能送到发价人地址,因为那天在发价人营业地是正式假日或非营业日,则接受期间应顺延至下一个营业日。

Article 20

(1) A period of time for acceptance fixed by the offeror in a telegram or a letter begins to run from the moment the telegram is handed in for dispatch or from the date shown on the letter or, if no such date is shown, from the date shown on the envelope. A period of time for acceptance fixed by the offeror by telephone, telex or other means of instantaneous communication, begins to run from the moment that the offer reaches the offeree.

(2) Official holidays or non-business days occurring during the period for acceptance are included in calculating the period. However, if a notice of acceptance can not be delivered at the address of the offeror on the last day of the period because that day falls on an official holiday or a non-business day at the place of business of the offeror, the period is extended until the first business day which follows.

第 21 条

(1)逾期接受仍有接受的效力,如果发价人毫不迟延地用口头或书面将此种意见通知被发价人。

(2)如果载有逾期接受的信件或其他书面文件表明,它是在传递正常、能及时送达发价人的情况下寄发的,则该项逾期接受具有接受的效力,除非发价人毫不迟延地用口头或书面通知被发价人:他认为他的发价已经失效。

Chapter 3　Business Negotiation

Article 21

(1) A late acceptance is nevertheless effective as an acceptance if without delay the offeror orally informs the offeree or dispatches a notice to that effect.

(2) If a letter or other writing containing a late acceptance shows that it has been sent in such circumstances that if its transmission had been normal, it would have reached the offeror in due time, the late acceptance is effective as an acceptance unless, without delay, the offeror orally informs the offeree that he considers his offer as having lapsed or dispatches a notice to that effect.

第 22 条

接受得予撤回,如果撤回通知于接受原应生效之前或同时送达发价人。

Article 22

An acceptance may be withdrawn if the withdrawal reaches the offeror before or at the same time as the acceptance would have become effective.

第 23 条

合同于按照本公约规定对发价的接受生效时订立。

Article 23

A contract is concluded at the moment when an acceptance of an offer becomes effective in accordance with the provisions of this convention.

第 24 条

为公约本部分的目的,发价、接受声明或任何其他意旨表示"送达"对方,系指用口头通知对方或通过任何其他方法送交对方本人,或其营业地或通讯地址,如无营业地或通讯地址,则送交对方惯常居住地。

Article 24

For the purposes of this part of the convention, an offer, declaration of acceptance or any other indication of intention "reaches" the addressee when it is made orally to him or delivered by any other means to him personally, to his place of business or mailing address or, if he does not have a place of business or mailing address, to his habitual residence.

Exercise

Ⅰ. *Multiple choice*

1. 某出口公司对外报盘某产品,根据《公约》的规定,下列哪种情况下,一经受盘人有效接受,双方即可达成交易(　　)。
   A. 发盘中只规定了商品的名称、数量及价格,同时向 A、B 两个公司发出
   B. 发盘中规定了各项交易条件,同时注明"以我方最后确认为准"
   C. 发盘中规定了各项交易条件,但并未规定成交的数量
   D. 发盘以平邮方式发出,但在当天发盘人又以传真方式要求撤回发盘

2. 根据《公约》的规定,下列说法中,不属于构成有效发盘条件的是(　　)。
   A. 必须规定有效期　　　　　　　B. 必须向一个特定的人做出
   C. 必须包括各项交易条件　　　　D. 有订立合同的意旨

3. 根据《公约》的规定,发盘内容必须十分确定,所谓十分确定,指在发盘中应包括下列要素(　　)。
   A. 货物的名称　　　　　　　　　B. 货物数量或规定数量的方法
   C. 货物的价格或规定确定价格的方法　　D. 交货时间与地点

4. 以下哪些是构成发盘的要件(　　)。
   A. 发盘内容明确　　　　　　　　B. 表明是不可撤销的、一定执行的
   C. 表明一旦对方接受即受其约束　　D. 必须向特定人发出的

5. 某项发盘于某月 12 日以电报形式送达受盘人,但在此之前的 11 日,发盘人以传真告知受盘人无效,此行为属于(　　)。
   A. 发盘的撤回　　B. 发盘的修改　　C. 一项新发盘　　D. 发盘的撤销

6. 根据《公约》的规定,下列哪些情况下发盘失效(　　)。
   A. 受盘人做出还盘　　　　　　　B. 发盘人在发盘规定的有效期内表示撤销原发盘
   C. 发盘有效期届满　　　　　　　D. 发盘被接受前,原发盘人破产

7. 我公司对某外商 A 就某产品发盘,下列哪种情况下,双方可达成交易(　　)。
   A. A 商在发盘有效期内,表示完全接受我公司发盘
   B. 由 A 商认可的 B 商在发盘有效期内向我公司表示完全接受发盘内容
   C. A 商根据以往经验,在未收到我发盘的情况下,向我公司表示接受
   D. A 商在有效期内表示接受,但提议将装运日期提前

8. 根据《公约》的规定,受盘人对下列哪些内容提出添加或更改,均作为实质性变更发盘条件(　　)。
   A. 价格　　　　　B. 付款　　　　　C. 品质　　　　　D. 数量

9. 卖方发盘限15日复到有效,14日下午收到买方复电要求减价3%并修改交货期,正研究如何答复时,次日上午又收到买方来电接受发盘(　　)。
   A. 于是,合同按卖方发盘条件达成　　　B. 于是,合同按买方提出条件达成
   C. 于是,合同按买方还实盘条件达成　　D. 此时,合同尚未达成

10. 根据《公约》的规定,受盘人对发盘表示接受,可以有几种方式。下列哪项不属此列(　　)?
    A. 通过口头向发盘人声明　　　　　　B. 通过书面形式向发盘人声明
    C. 通过沉默或不行动表示接受　　　　D. 通过实际行动表示接受

11. 关于逾期接受,《公约》规定(　　)。
    A. 逾期接受无效　　　　　　　　　　B. 逾期接受是一个新的发盘
    C. 逾期接受完全无效　　　　　　　　D. 逾期接受是否有效,关键看发盘人如何表态

12. 一项接受由于电讯部门的延误,发盘人收到此项接受时已经超过了该发盘的有效期,则(　　)。
    A. 除非发盘人及时提出异议,该逾期接受有效
    B. 只要发盘人及时表示确认,该逾期接受有效
    C. 该逾期接受丧失接受效力
    D. 该逾期接受有效

II. *Translate the following sentences*

1. In view of our longstanding business relations, we can consider a price reduction.

2. We regret to say that your quotation is out of line with the prevailing market at this end.

3. This corporation specializes in importing textiles.

4. Your firm has been recommended to us by the Chamber of Commerce in Tokyo, Japan.

5. We are convinced that with joint efforts business between us will be developed to our mutual benefit.

6. It will be greatly appreciated if you will give us your cooperation.

7. We are striving to expand economic cooperation and exchange of technology with foreign countries, and will utilize common and reasonable international practices in a flexible way.

8. 遗憾,即使各让一半,我们仍难以接受你方还盘。

9. 在质量方面,我们认为其他品牌的产品是无法与我们相比的。

10. 我们每年对金属配件的需求量是相当大的。如果你们的价格具有竞争力,交货迅速,我们可能大量订购。

11. 该报盘以商品未售出为准。

12. 我们已按你方要求将报盘延期。

13. 此报盘着眼于扩大销路而且很有竞争性。

14. 当事人应当遵循公平原则来确定各方的权利和义务。

15. 当事人行使权利、履行义务应当遵循诚实信用的原则。

16. 委托合同是委托人和受托人约定,由受托人处理委托人事务的合同。

17. 装船通知:卖方应于货物装船完毕后,立即以电报通知买方合同号、货物名称、数量、毛重、发票金额、船名和起航日期。若由于卖方未及时以电报通知买方,而使买方不能按时办理保险时,由此产生的一切损失,均应由卖方承担。

Ⅲ. *True or false*
1. An advertisement is an offer.
2. Withdrawal happens before the offer becomes effective while revocation happens after the offer becomes effective.
3. The offeror must fix a period of time for acceptance in the offer.
4. An oral acceptance can be effective.
5. A price list is an offer.

6. An acceptance can be made by performing an act.

Ⅳ. *Term definition*
1. revocation of an offer
2. non-firm offer
3. withdrawal of offer
4. material alteration

Ⅴ. *Case study*
1. A Company in Shanghai quotes its exporting price, USD 50.00 Per case CFR C3% Kuwait. But the foreign company requires the Shanghai exporter to offer FOB Shanghai net price. If the standard of calculating basic freight of the exporting goods is "W/M", the measurement of a case with goods is 42×28×25 cubic centimeters and it's gross weight is 0.2 Metric Ton, the basic freight rate for the goods is USD 70.00 per freight ton.

   Does the requirement made by the foreign company constitute an acceptance? Why?

2. 甲方于4月5日发信函给乙方,内容如下:我厂现有1000台飞人自行车,售价为CIF 200元/台,若有意请在10天内答复。乙方于4月8日收到该信函。
   (1)甲方于4月5日给乙方所发信函是否构成发盘?

   (2)4月10日回复同意甲方条件但要求改为FOB价格,则乙方回复是否构成有效接受?为什么?合同是否成立?

   (3)4月10日回复同意甲方条件但要求增加交易中单据的份数,甲方回电表明不同意,则乙方回复是否构成有效接受?为什么?合同是否成立?

   (4)4月7日自行车市场价格上浮,甲方立即电话通知乙方修改价格为240元/台,则甲方行为是否有效?

   (5)4月9日自行车市场价格上浮,甲方立即通知乙方撤销原发盘,此时乙方并未对甲方信函做答复,则甲方行为是否有效?

(6) 乙方于 4 月 8 日收到该信函后,没有立即答复,4 月 16 日自行车市场价格上浮,甲方 4 月 17 日收到乙方愿意接受的回复,则合同是否成立?

(7) 乙方于 4 月 8 日收到该信函后,没有立即答复,甲方于 4 月 18 日收到乙方愿意接受的回复,若甲方收到回复后,立即致电表明择日签约的意思,则合同是否成立?

(8) 乙方于 4 月 8 日收到该信函后,没有立即答复,甲方于 4 月 18 日收到乙方愿意接受的回复,若甲方收到回复后,自行车市场价格上浮,甲方表明不接受乙方的回复,则合同是否成立?

(9) 乙方于 4 月 8 日收到该信函后,没有立即答复,甲方于 4 月 18 日收到乙方愿意接受的回复,则合同是否成立?

3. 甲出口公司向国外乙公司报价:小麦 500 公吨,每公吨 260 美元,发盘有效期 6 天。乙公司两天后回复要求将货物价格降为每公吨 240 美元。4 天后,甲公司将这批小麦卖给了国外丙公司,并在第六天告知乙公司货物已售他人。乙公司认为甲公司违约,要求甲公司赔偿。问:甲公司是否应赔偿乙公司?说明理由。

Ⅵ. *Write a letter of offer according to the information given below*

中国国家工艺品进出口有限公司收到苏丹贸易有限公司 5 月 12 号的询问关于货号为 No. 512 款瓷器的询价信。现报虚盘如下:No. 512:USD 50 per dozen CIF C 5% Port Sudan,数量为 3400 dozens,支付方式为保兑不可撤销信用证,要求立即装运,并根据对方要求另寄样品。

Chapter 4　Quality, Quantity and Packing of Goods

Quality
  ways of expressing quality
  quality tolerance
  quality clauses in contract
Quantity
  calculation of quantity
  calculation of weight
  more or less clause
Packing
  shipping marks

4.1　Ways of Expressing Quality

　　The seller must deliver goods that are of the quality required by the contract. The qualities of different commodities can be expressed in different ways. In international trade, the ways of expressing quality of commodity may fall into two types: by sample and by description.

4.1.1　Sale by sample

　　For goods whose qualities are hard to describe, samples are needed to express the qualities. Sale by sample can be divided into "sale by seller's sample" and "sale by buyer's sample". Under this method, the seller is responsible for delivering the goods with the same quality as samples.

(1) Sale by seller's Sample

Duplicate Sample

(2) Sale by buyer's sample

Tips：

① By seller's sample, the sample should be representative.

② The seller should keep duplicate sample.

③ Flexible clause.

④ By buyer's sample, it should be changed into "return sample" or "counter sample".

Case study：

我方与越南某客商凭样品成交达成一笔出口镰刀的交易。合同中规定复验有效期为货物到达目的港后的60天。货物到目的港经越商复验后，未提出任何异议。但事隔半年，越商来电称：镰刀全部生锈，只能降价出售。越商因此要求我方按成交价格的40％赔偿其损失。我方接电后立即查看我方留存的复样，也发现类似情况。

问：我方应否同意对方的要求，为什么？

4.1.2 Sale by description

In export trade, it is proper to express the quality of most of goods by description. This method can be further classified into the following types：

(1) Sale by specification

Specification covers composition, content, purity, size, length, thickness, etc. The contents of specification vary with different characteristics of the qualities. It is frequently used in international trade because of its convenience and preciseness.

e.g. Chinese Soybean

  moisture(max)15％,

  oil content(min)17％,

  admixture(max)1％,

  imperfect granules(max)7％

Chapter 4 Quality, Quantity and Packing of Goods

(2) Sale by grade

When the method of "sale by grade" is used, the quality clause becomes simple, but the seller and the buyer should reach an agreement on the "grade".

(3) Sale by standard

Standards are those specifications that are laid down by government departments or commercial organizations of a country. There are many standard specifications in commodities. For example, there are terms like G. O. B or Good Ordinary Brand, F. A. Q or Fair Average Quality, and G. M. Q or Good Merchantable Quality.

(4) Sale by descriptions and illustrations

The qualities of some commodities like machines, instruments, electric appliances can not be described by merely indicating specifications. Therefore, technical manuals, booklets, drawings or diagrams are provided to express their qualities. For example,

品质和技术数据必须与买方提供的产品说明书严格相符。

Quality and technical data shall be strictly in conformity with the description submitted by the buyer.

(5) Sale by trade mark or brand name

(6) Sale by name of origin

4.1.3 Quality tolerance

Quality tolerance means the permissible range within which the quality supplied by the seller may be either superior or inferior to the quality stipulated in the contract. Sometimes, price adjustment is not needed if the tolerance is within certain limit.

e. g. B601 Tomato Paste 28/30 concentration

Grey duck feather down content 18%, 1% more or less.

Case study:

我某公司出口纺织原料一批,合同规定水分最高15%,杂质不超过3%,但在成交前曾向买方寄过样品,订约后,我方又电告对方成交货物与样品相似。货到后,买方提出货物的质量比样品低7%的检验证明,并要求我方赔偿损失。

问:我方是否该赔?为什么?

4.1.4　Quality clauses in contract

(1) Sample No. 518 Raincoat
(2) Chinese Northeast Soybean
　　　Moisture　　15% (Max.)
　　　Admixture　　1% (Max.)
　　　Imperfect Granules　7% (Max.)
　　　Oil Content　17% (Min.)
(3) Quality and technical data to be in conformity with the attached technical agreement which forms an integral part of this contract.

4.2　Quantity

The business laws of some countries stipulate that the quantity of the goods should be in conformity with that agreed in the contract. According to *United Nations Convention on Contracts for Sale of Goods*, if the seller delivers a quantity of goods greater than that required in the contract, the buyer may take delivery or refuse to take delivery of the excess part. If the buyer takes delivery of all or the excess part, he must pay for it at the contract price.

4.2.1　Calculation of quantity

Units of measurement

weight	gram, kilogram, ounce, pound, metric ton, long ton, short ton
number	piece, package, pair, set, dozen, gross, ream
length	meter, centimeter, foot, yard
area	square meter, square foot, square yard
volume	cubic meter, cubic centimeter, cubic foot, cubic yard
capacity	liter, gallon, pint, bushel

4.2.2 Calculation of weight

Weight can be calculated in the following ways:

(1) By gross weight

(2) By net weight

It is customary to calculate the weight by net weight if the contract doesn't stipulate definitely by gross weight or by net weight.

(3) By conditioned weight

Conditioned weight is obtained with the actual moisture content of the goods removed by scientific method and the standardized moisture added. It is often used for such commodities as raw silk, cotton and wool, which are of high economic value and with unsteady moisture content.

Question: If the contract doesn't stipulate definitely by gross weight or by net weight, how would the weight be calculated?

The formula of calculating the conditioned weight:

Conditioned weight = actual weight × (1 + standard regaining rate of water) / (1 + actual regaining rate of water)

Question: 我一服装加工厂从澳大利亚进口羊毛20公吨,双方约定标准回潮率为11%,若测得该批羊毛的实际回潮率为25%,则该批羊毛的公量应为多少?

4.2.3 More or less clause

For a quantity clause, such expressions as "about/approximately" should be avoided because these words may rouse disputes. Both parties generally agree to use "more or less clause" in order to facilitate the processing of business. A complete "more or less clause" should contain the following:

(1) Permissible range.

(2) Option.

(3) Pricing method of excess or shortage.

e.g. 数量:100公吨,2%上下,由卖方决定,多交或不足部分按合同价格计算。

Quantity: 100 metric tons with 2% more or less at seller's option, such excess or shortage to be settled at contractual price.

e. g. China White Tea 50 metric tons with 5％ more or less at seller's option in order to meet the shipping space and the difference to be settled at the CIF contract price.

中国茶叶50公吨,卖方有权在合同规定的数量基础上多装或少装5％,视船舱容量而定,溢短装的差额部分按CIF合同价计算。

Case study：

做过很多信用证,习惯了都是＋/－10％的溢短装,现在有份信用证居然没有这个条款,结果货多出了,金额也多了,不过是在10％范围内的,这样算不符吗?

提示：Article 30 of UCP 600

A tolerance not to exceed 5％ more or 5％ less than the quantity of the goods is allowed, provided the credit does not state the quantity in terms of a stipulated number of packing units or individual items and the total amount of the drawings does not exceed the amount of the credit.

4.3　Packing

Shipping Mark　Shipping marks are marks of simple designs, some letters, numbers and simple words on packages which serve as an identification of the consignment to which they belong. The shipping marks consist of, for example：

TMCO	（收货人）
NEW YORK	（目的地或目的港）
2003/C NO.56	（合同、订单、发票号码）
NO.1-30	（件号）

UCP 600-Article 30　Tolerance in Credit Amount, Quantity and Unit Prices

a. The words "about" or "approximately" used in connection with the amount of the credit or the quantity or the unit price stated in the credit are to be construed as allowing a tolerance not to exceed 10％ more or 10％ less than the amount, the quantity or the unit price to which they refer.

b. A tolerance not to exceed 5％ more or 5％ less than the quantity of the

Chapter 4 Quality, Quantity and Packing of Goods

goods is allowed, provided the credit does not state the quantity in terms of a stipulated number of packing units or individual items and the total amount of the drawings does not exceed the amount of the credit.

c. Even when partial shipments are not allowed, a tolerance not to exceed 5% less than the amount of the credit is allowed, provided that the quantity of the goods, if stated in the credit, is shipped in full and a unit price, if stated in the credit, is not reduced or that sub-article 30 (b) is not applicable. This tolerance does not apply when the credit stipulates a specific tolerance or uses the expressions referred to in sub-article 30 (a).

UCP 600 第 30 条　信用证金额、数量与单价的增减幅度

a. "约"或"大约"用于信用证金额、数量或单价时,应解释为允许有关金额、数量或单价有不超过 10% 的增减幅度。

b. 在信用证未以包装单位件数或货物自身件数的方式规定货物数量时,货物数量允许有 5% 的增减幅度,只要总支取金额不超过信用证金额。

c. 如果信用证规定了货物数量,且该数量已全部发运,以及当信用证规定了单价,而该单价又未降低时,或当第 30 条 b 款不适用时,则即使不允许部分装运,也允许支取的金额有 5% 的减幅。若信用证规定有特定的增减幅度或使用第 30 条 a 款提到的用语限定数量,则该减幅不适用。

Exercise

Ⅰ. *Blank filling*

1. 良好平均品质英文(　　　)缩写(　　　)。
2. 货物皮重的计算包括(　　　)。
3. 包装标志包括(　　　)。
4. 在买卖合同中的溢短装条款中,如果对溢短装部分规定作价办法,按惯例应该按(　　　)价格结算。
5. 国际贸易中惯常用来表示商品品质的方法包括(　　　)和(　　　)两类。
6. 采用净重计算时,关键是如何计算(　　　)的重量。
7. 短装条款主要包括(　　　)、(　　　)以及(　　　)。
8. 按其在流通领域中所起的作用的不同,商品包装可分为(　　　)和(　　　)。
9. 运输包装上的标志按其用途可分为(　　　)、(　　　)和(　　　)。
10. 复验期限规定越长,卖方承担风险就越(　　　)。

Ⅱ. *Multiple choice.*

1. 凭样品成交的基本要求是（　　）。
   A. 样品作为交货的唯一依据　　　　B. 卖方所交货物必须与样品一致
   C. 货物和样品之间可以存在差异　　D. 样品成交以买方为主
2. 计算皮重的几种方法包括（　　）。
   A. 习惯皮重　　B. 约定皮重　　C. 实际皮重　　D. 合同皮重　　E. 平均皮重
3. 出口羊毛计算重量通常采用（　　）。
   A. 毛重　　　　B. 净重　　　　C. 公量　　　　D. 以毛作净
4. 国外来证规定，交货数量为 10 000 公吨散装货，未表明可否溢短装，不准分批装运，根据《UCP600》规定，卖方发货的（　　）。
   A. 数量和总金额均可增减 10%　　　B. 数量和总金额均可增减 5%
   C. 数量可增减 5%，总金额不可超过　D. 总金额可增减 5%，数量不可超过
5. 对于溢短装部分的作价方法，合同中如果没有明确的规定，按照惯例其做法是（　　）。
   A. 按合同价格作价　　　　　　　　B. 按装船时的国际市场价格作价
   C. 按到货时的国际市场价格作价
6. 合同重的数量条款为"1000M/T with 5% more or less at seller's option"则卖方交货数量可以是（　　）。
   A. 950 M/T　　　　　　B. 1000M/T　　　　　　C. 1050M/T
   D. 1500M/T　　　　　　E. 950 M/T 到 1050M/T 之间任何数量
7. 国际标准化组织推荐的标准运输标志，应该包括（　　）。
   A. 收货人名称的缩写或简称　　　　B. 参考号（订单、发票号）
   C. 目的地　　　D. 件号或箱号　　　E. 产地标志
8. "标的物"条款就是合同的（　　）。
   A. 品质条款　　B. 数量条款　　C. 品名条款　　D. 说明条款
9. 适用于在造型上有特殊要求或具有色、香、味方面特征的商品，表示品质的方式是（　　）。
   A. 凭等级买卖　　B. 凭样品买卖　　C. 凭商标买卖　　D. 凭说明书买卖
10. 在国际贸易中，对以重量计量的商品的计价，使用最多的计量方法是（　　）。
    A. 毛重　　　　B. 净重　　　　C. 理论重量　　　D. 法定重量
11. 在国际贸易中，对于大宗低值的农产品，通常采用的计量办法是（　　）。
    A. 毛重　　　　B. 净重　　　　C. 公量　　　　D. 以毛作净
12. 在国际贸易中，对生丝、羊毛、棉花等有较强吸湿性的商品，其计量办法通常为（　　）。

Chapter 4　Quality, Quantity and Packing of Goods

　　A. 毛重　　　　　B. 净重　　　　　C. 公量　　　　　D. 理论重量

13. 国际商会《跟单信用证统一惯例》600 号出版物对于"约量"的解释幅度为不超过（　　）。

　　A. 3％　　　　　B. 5％　　　　　C. 10％　　　　　D. 15％

14. 按国际惯例，买卖商品按重量计价时，如果合同中未明确规定计量方法，应按（　　）。

　　A. 毛重　　　　　B. 净重　　　　　C. 理论重量　　　　　D. 法定重量

15. 按照国际贸易惯例，如果合同中没有相关规定，则运输标志的提供方一般是（　　）。

　　A. 开证行　　　　　B. 卖方　　　　　C. 买方　　　　　D. 船方

16. 根据《联合国国际货物销售合同公约》的规定，买方如果收取了卖方多交的货物，则多收部分货物的计价应按（　　）。

　　A. 合同价　　　　　　　　　　B. 装船日的市场价格
　　C. 到货日的市场价格　　　　　D. 双方议定

17. 国际上应用较广泛的商品检验时间、地点的规定方法是（　　）。

　　A. 装船前装运港检验
　　B. 出口国装运港（地）检验，进口国目的港（地）复验
　　C. 装运港（地）检验重量，目的港（地）检验品质
　　D. 进口国目的港（地）检验

18. 在下列各项中，不属于商检证书作用的是（　　）。

　　A. 作为索赔和理赔的依据之一　　　B. 作为仲裁机构受理案件的依据之一
　　C. 作为银行付款的单据之一　　　　D. 作为海关验关放行的依据之一

19. 国际标准化组织的英文缩写是（　　）。

　　A. ISO　　　　　B. UL　　　　　C. IWS　　　　　D. SGS

20. 以实物表示商品品质的方法有（　　）。

　　A. 看货买卖　　　B. 凭样品买卖　　　C. 凭价格买卖　　　D. 凭等级买卖

21. 对等样品也被称为（　　）。

　　A. 复样　　　　　B. 回样　　　　　C. 确认样　　　　　D. 卖方样品

22. 在国际贸易中，如果卖方交货数量多于合同规定的数量，根据《联合国国际货物销售合同公约》的规定，买方可以（　　）。

　　A. 接受全部货物　　　　　　　B. 拒绝全部货物
　　C. 拒绝多交的货物　　　　　　D. 接受多交货物中的一部分

23. 运输包装上的标志，按其作用或用途可分为（　　）。

　　A. 运输标志　　　B. 指示性标志　　　C. 警告性标志　　　D. 条形码

24. 按照国际标准化组织的建议和推荐,标准运输标志的内容包括(　　)。
    A. 收货人的英文缩写字母或简称　　　B. 参考号
    C. 目的地　　　　　　　　　　　　D. 件数号码
25. 商品检验证书在国际贸易中的作用是(　　)。
    A. 证明卖方所交货物是否符合合同规定的依据　　B. 对外索赔的依据
    C. 通关放行的有效证件　　　　　　　　　　　　D. 银行付款的主要依据

Ⅲ. True or false statements

1. 采用凭样品成交时,为了争取国外客户,应选择质量最好的样品给对方,以达成交易。(　　)
2. 根据品质公差条款的规定,只要卖方所交货物在品质公差范围内,买方不得拒收,也不得要求调整价格。(　　)
3. 根据《联合国国际货物销售合同公约》规定,如果卖方所交货物多于合同规定数量,买方可拒收全部货物。(　　)
4. 国际贸易中,如一方违反合同的包装条款,另一方只能提出损害赔偿,但无权拒收货物.(　　)
5. 对棉花、生丝等商品一般采用公量计算其重量。(　　)
6. 销售包装的主要作用在于保护商品,以防在储运过程中发生货损货差。(　　)
7. 中性包装的使用主要是为了避免一些关税及非关税壁垒。(　　)
8. 运输包装上的标志就是指运输标志,也就是通常所说的唛头。(　　)
9. 合同中必须规定溢短装条款。(　　)
10. 溢短装条款是在装运输数量上可增减一定幅度,该增减既可由卖方决定,也可以由买方决定,应该看合同中的具体规定而定。(　　)
11. 按照重量计算的包装货,如果买卖合同没有明确规定是按照毛重计算或者按照净重计算,则按照惯例,应该按照毛重计算。(　　)
12. 在约定的品质机动幅度和品质公差范围内的品质差异,除非另有规定,一般不另行规定增减价格。(　　)
13. 为了适应国际市场需要,我们出口日用工业品,应该尽量争取按照买方样品达成交易。(　　)
14. 在出口贸易中,表示商品的品质方法很多,为了明确责任,最好采用凭样品买卖,又凭规格买卖的方法。(　　)

Ⅳ. Answering short questions

1. 简述凭样品买卖的基本类型、各自特点。

Chapter 4 Quality, Quantity and Packing of Goods

2. 运输包装中的运输标志的主要内容是什么？

3. 表示品质的方法有哪些？

4. 如卖方按每箱 150 美元的价格出售某商品 1000 箱，合同规定数量允许有 5％增减，由卖方决定。试问：(1)这是一个什么条款？(2)最多可装多少箱？最少可装多少箱？(3)如实际装运 1040 箱，买方应付货款多少？

5. 什么叫唛头？为什么要在商品的外包装上刷制唛头？它一般由哪些部分组成？

6. 在出口贸易中，表示品质的方法多种多样，为了明确责任，最好采用既凭样品又凭规格买卖的做法。你认为这样的做法对否？为什么？

V. *Case study*

1. 在合同中规定：about 100 M/T 或 100 M/T，5％ more or less at seller's option 条款，有无不同？在后一种情况下，卖方最多和最少可交货多少公吨？

2. 中国某公司从国外进口某农产品，合同数量为 100 万吨，允许溢短 5％，而外商装船时共装运了 120 万吨，对多装的 15 万吨，我方应如何处理？

3. 我国某出口公司对外出口一批罐头，合同规定数量为 454g×24 听纸箱 1000 箱。我方根据库存情况，实际出口 454 克×48 听纸箱装 500 箱。外商以我方包装不符为由拒收货物。问：外商拒收是否有理？为什么？

Chapter 5 Incoterms

Functions of trade terms
EXW, FCA, CPT, CIP, DAP, DAT, DDP
FAS, FOB, CFR, CIF
Calculation of quotation

5.1 Functions of Trade Terms

5.1.1 Components of trade terms

In international trade, the unit price consists of type of currency, price per unit, measurement unit and trade terms. For example, a price term, "₤ 100 per M/T CIF London", may be described as follows:

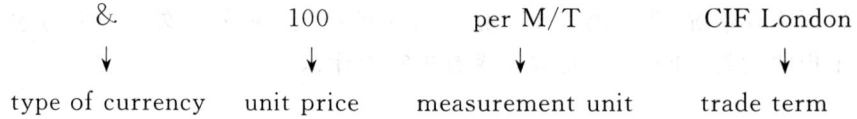

5.1.2 Functions of trade terms

The purpose of Incoterms (International Rules for the Interpretation of Trade Terms) is to provide a set of international rules for the interpretation of the most commonly used trade terms in foreign trade. The trade terms are used to explain the price composition, to define the delivery point, to indicate which party should bear the freight, insurance, and undertake the risks in case damage to or loss of the goods occurs. In a word, trade terms stipulate both parties responsibilities under a transaction.

5.2 Terms for Any Mode of Transport

The terms under Incoterms 2010 are classified into two major groups, which is different from Incoterms 2000. The terms in the first group can be used for any mode of transport, which contain EXW, FCA, CPT, CIP, DAP, DAT and DDP. The terms in the second group can only be used for sea or inland waterway transport, which contain FAS, FOB, CFR and CIF.

5.2.1 EXW (EX WORKS)

This term means the seller fulfills his obligation to deliver when he has made the goods available at his own premises to the buyer. He is not responsible for clearing the goods for export, unless otherwise agreed. This term represents the minimum obligation for the seller.

Seller's obligation	Buyer's obligation
①Place the goods at the disposal of the buyer at the named place of delivery. ② Provide appropriate packing and marking. ③ Assist the buyer with the export documentation.	①Take delivery of the goods within the agreed period at the agreed place and pay the price as provided in the contract of sale. ②Bear all costs and risks to the goods after they are delivered. ③Obtain at his own risk and expense any import and export license or other official authorization and carry out all customs formalities necessary for the import and export of the goods.

5.2.2 FCA (FREE CARRIER) (insert named place of delivery) Incoterms 2010

This term may be used irrespective of the mode of transport selected and may also be used where more than one mode of transport is employed. "Free Carrier" means that the seller delivers the goods to the carrier or another person nominated by the buyer at the seller's premises or another named place. The parties are well advised to specify as clearly as possible the point within the named place of delivery, as the risk passes to the buyer at that point. If the parties intend to deliver the goods at the seller's premises, they should identify the address of those premises as the named place of delivery. If, on the other hand, the parties intend the goods to be delivered at another place, they must identify a different specific place of delivery.

FCA requires the seller to clear the goods for export, where applicable. However, the seller has no obligation to clear the goods for import, pay any import duty or carry out any import customs formalities.

Seller's obligation	Buyer's obligation
①Place the goods at the disposal of the carrier at the named place. ② Provide appropriate packing and marking. ③Carry out the export formalities and provide the buyer with the document received for the delivery of the goods.	① Take delivery of the goods within the agreed period at the agreed place and pay the price as provided in the contract of sale. ②Bear all costs and risks to the goods after they are delivered. ③Carry out the import formalities and contract of carriage to the final destination.

5.2.3 CPT (CARRIAGE PAID TO) (insert named place of destination) Incoterms 2010

This rule may be used irrespective of the mode of transport selected and may also be used where more than one mode of transport is employed.

"Carriage Paid To" means that the seller delivers the goods to the carrier or another person nominated by the seller at an agreed place (if any such place is agreed between the parties) and that the seller must contract for and pay the costs of carriage necessary to bring the goods to the named place of destination.

When CPT, CIP, CFR or CIF are used, the seller fulfills its obligation to deliver when it hands the goods over to the carrier and not when the goods reach the place of destination.

This rule has two critical points, because risk passes and costs are transferred at different places. The parties are well advised to identify as precisely as possible in the contract both the place of delivery, where the risk passes to the buyer, and the named place of destination to which the seller must contract for the carriage. If several carriers are used for the carriage to the agreed destination and the parties do not agree on a specific point of delivery, the default position is that risk passes when the goods have been delivered to the first carrier at a point entirely of the seller's choosing and over which the buyer has no control. Should the parties wish the risk to pass at a later stage (e.g., at an ocean port or airport), they need to specify this in their contract of sale. The parties are also well advised to identify as precisely as possible the point within the agreed place of destination, as the costs to that point are for the account of the seller. The seller is advised to procure contracts of carriage that match this choice precisely. If the seller incurs costs under its contract of carriage related to unloading at the named place of destination, the seller is not entitled to recover such costs from the buyer unless otherwise agreed between the parties. CPT requires the seller to clear the goods for export, where applicable. However, the seller has no obligation to clear the goods for import, pay any import duty or carry out any import customs formalities.

5.2.4 CIP (CARRIAGE AND INSURANCE PAID TO) (insert named place of destination) Incoterms 2010

This rule may be used irrespective of the mode of transport selected and may also be used where more than one mode of transport is employed. "Carriage and Insurance Paid to" means that the seller delivers the goods to the carrier or another person nominated by the seller at an agreed place (if any such place is agreed between the parties) and that the seller must contract for and pay the costs of carriage necessary to bring the goods to the named place of destination.

The seller also contracts for insurance cover against the buyer's risk of loss of or damage to the goods during the carriage. The buyer should note that under CIP the seller is required to obtain insurance only on minimum cover. Should the buyer wish to have more insurance protection, it will need either to agree as much expressly with the seller or to make its own extra insurance arrangements.

When CPT, CIP, CFR or CIF are used, the seller fulfills its obligation to deliver when it hands the goods over to the carrier and when the goods don't reach the place of destination.

This rule has two critical points, because risk passes and costs are transferred at different places. The parties are well advised to identify as precisely as possible in the contract both the place of delivery, where the risk passes to the buyer, and the named place of destination to which the seller must contract for carriage. If several carriers are used for the carriage to the agreed destination and the parties do not agree on a specific point of delivery, the default position is that risk passes when the goods have been delivered to the first carrier at a point entirely of the seller's choosing and over which the buyer has no control. Should the parties wish the risk to pass at a later stage (e. g., at an ocean port or an airport), they need to specify this in their contract of sale.

The parties are also well advised to identify as precisely as possible the point within the agreed place of destination, as the costs to that point are for the account of the seller. The seller is advised to procure contracts of carriage that match this choice precisely. If the seller incurs costs under its contract of carriage related to unloading at the named place of destination, the seller is not entitled to recover such costs from the buyer unless otherwise agreed between the parties. CIP requires the seller to clear the goods for export, where applicable. However, the seller has no obligation to clear the goods for import, pay any import duty or carry out any import customs formalities.

5.2.5　DAT(DELIVERED AT TERMINAL)(insert named terminal at port or place of destination) Incoterms 2010

This rule may be used irrespective of the mode of transport selected and may also be used where more than one mode of transport is employed.

"Delivered at Terminal" means that the seller delivers when the goods, once unloaded from the arriving means of transport, are placed at the disposal of the buyer at a named terminal at the named port or place of destination. "Terminal" includes any place, whether covered or not, such as a quay, warehouse, container yard or road, rail or air cargo terminal.

The seller bears all risks involved in bringing the goods to and unloading them at the terminal at the named port or place of destination. The parties are well advised to specify as clearly as possible the terminal and, if possible, a specific point within the terminal at the agreed port or place of destination, as the risks to that point are for the account of the seller. The seller is advised to procure a contract of carriage that matches this choice precisely. Moreover, if the parties intend the seller to bear the risks and costs involved in transporting and handling the goods from the terminal to another place, then the DAP or DDP rules should be used.

DAT requires the seller to clear the goods for export, where applicable. However, the seller has no obligation to clear the goods for import, pay any import duty or carry out any import customs formalities.

A THE SELLER'S OBLIGATIONS

A1 General obligations of the seller

The seller must provide the goods and the commercial invoice in conformity with the contract of sale and any other evidence of conformity that may be required by the contract. Any document referred to in A1-A10 may be an equivalent electronic record or procedure if agreed between the parties or customary.

A2 Licenses, authorizations, security clearances and other formalities

Where applicable, the seller must obtain, at its own risk and expense, any export license and other official authorization and carry out all customs formalities necessary for the export of the goods and for their transport through any country prior to delivery.

A3 Contracts of carriage and insurance

(a) Contract of carriage

The seller must contract at its own expense for the carriage of the goods to the named terminal at the agreed port or place of destination. If a specific terminal is not agreed or is not determined by practice, the seller may select the terminal at the agreed port or place of destination that best suits its purpose.

(b) Contract of insurance

The seller has no obligation to the buyer to make a contract of insurance. However, the seller must provide the buyer, at the buyer's request, risk and expense (if any), with information that the buyer needs for obtaining insurance.

A4 Delivery

The seller must unload the goods from the arriving means of transport and must then deliver them by placing them at the disposal of the buyer at the named terminal referred to in A3 (a) at the port or place of destination on the agreed date or within the agreed period.

B THE BUYER'S OBLIGATIONS

B1 General obligations of the buyer

The buyer must pay the price of the goods as provided in the contract of sale.

Any document referred to in B1-B10 may be an equivalent electronic record or procedure if agreed between the parties or customary.

B2 Licenses, authorizations, security clearances and other formalities

Where applicable, the buyer must obtain, at its own risk and expense, any import license or other official authorization and carry out all customs formalities for the import of the goods.

B3 Contracts of carriage and insurance

(a) Contract of carriage

The buyer has no obligation to the seller to make a contract of carriage.

(b) Contract of insurance

The buyer has no obligation to the seller to make a contract of insurance. However, the buyer must provide the seller, upon request, with the necessary information for obtaining insurance.

B4 Taking delivery

The buyer must take delivery of the goods when they have been delivered as envisaged in A4.

A5 Transfer of risks

The seller bears all risks of loss of or damage to the goods until they have been delivered in accordance with A4 with the exception of loss or damage in the circumstances described in B5.

A6 Allocation of costs

The seller must pay:

(a) In addition to costs resulting from A3 (a), all costs relating to the goods until they have been delivered in accordance with A4, other than those payable by the buyer as envisaged in B6; and

(b) Where applicable, the costs of customs formalities necessary for export as well as all duties, taxes and other charges payable upon export and the costs for their transport through any country, prior to delivery in accordance with A4.

A7　Notices to the buyer

The seller must give the buyer any notice needed in order to allow the buyer to take measures that are normally necessary to enable the buyer to take delivery of the goods.

A8　Delivery document

The seller must provide the buyer, at the seller's expense, with a document enabling the buyer to take delivery of the goods as envisaged in A4/B4.

B5　Transfer of risks

The buyer bears all risks of loss of or damage to the goods from the time they have been delivered as envisaged in A4. If

(a) The buyer fails to fulfill its obligations in accordance with B2, then it bears all resulting risks of loss of or damage to the goods; or

(b) The buyer fails to give notice in accordance with B7, then it bears all risks of loss of or damage to the goods from the agreed date or the expiry date of the agreed period for delivery, provided that the goods have been clearly identified as the contract goods.

B6　Allocation of costs

The buyer must pay

(a) All costs relating to the goods from the time they have been delivered as envisaged in A4;

(b) Any additional costs incurred by the seller if the buyer fails to fulfill its obligations in accordance with B2, or to give notice in accordance with B7, provided that the goods have been clearly identified as the contract goods; and

(c) Where applicable, the costs of customs formalities as well as all duties, taxes and other charges payable upon import of the goods.

B7   Notices to the seller

The buyer must, whenever it is entitled to determine the time within an agreed period and/or the point of taking delivery at the named terminal, give the seller sufficient notice thereof.

B8   Proof of delivery

The buyer must accept the delivery document provided as envisaged in A8.

A9   Checking – packaging – marking

The seller must pay the costs of those checking operations (such as checking quality, measuring, weighing, counting) that are necessary for the purpose of delivering the goods in accordance with A4, as well as the costs of any pre-shipment inspection mandated by the authority of the country of export. The seller must, at its own expense, package the goods, unless it is usual for the particular trade to transport the type of goods sold unpackaged. The seller may package the goods in the manner appropriate for their transport, unless the buyer has notified the seller of specific packaging requirements before the contract of sale is concluded. Packaging is to be marked appropriately.

A10   Assistance with information and related costs

The seller must, where applicable, in a timely manner, provide to or render assistance in obtaining for the buyer, at the buyer's request, risk and expense, any documents and information, including security-related information, that the buyer needs for the import of the goods and/or for their transport to the final destination.

The seller must reimburse the buyer for all costs and charges incurred by the buyer in providing or rendering assistance in obtaining documents and information as envisaged in B10.

B9   Inspection of goods

The buyer must pay the costs of any mandatory pre-shipment inspection, except when such inspection is mandated by the authorities of the country of export.

B10 Assistance with information and related costs

The buyer must, in a timely manner, advise the seller of any security information requirements so that the seller may comply with A10.

The buyer must reimburse the seller for all costs and charges incurred by the seller in providing or rendering assistance in obtaining documents and information as envisaged in A10.

The buyer must, where applicable, in a timely manner, provide to or render assistance in obtaining for the seller, at the seller's request, risk and expense, any documents and information, including security-related information, that the seller needs for the transport and export of the goods and for their transport through any country.

5.2.6 DAP (DELIVERED AT PLACE) (insert named place of destination) Incoterms 2010

This rule may be used irrespective of the mode of transport selected and may also be used where more than one mode of transport is employed.

"Delivered at Place" means that the seller delivers when the goods are placed at the disposal of the buyer on the arriving means of transport ready for unloading at the named place of destination. The seller bears all risks involved in bringing the goods to the named place.

The parties are well advised to specify as clearly as possible the point within the agreed place of destination, as the risks to that point are for the account of the seller. The seller is advised to procure contracts of carriage that match this choice precisely. If the seller incurs costs under its contract of carriage related to unloading at the place of destination, the seller is not entitled to recover such costs from the buyer unless otherwise agreed between the parties. DAP requires the seller to clear the goods for export, where applicable.

However, the seller has no obligation to clear the goods for import, pay any import duty or carry out any import customs formalities. If the parties wish the seller to clear the goods for import, pay any import duty and carry out any import customs formalities, the DDP term should be used.

A THE SELLER'S OBLIGATIONS

A1   General obligations of the seller

The seller must provide the goods and the commercial invoice in conformity with the contract of sale and any other evidence of conformity that may be required by the contract. Any document referred to in A1-A10 may be an equivalent electronic record or procedure if agreed between the parties or customary.

A2   Licenses, authorizations, security clearances and other formalities

Where applicable, the seller must obtain, at its own risk and expense, any export license and other official authorization and carry out all customs formalities necessary for the export of the goods and for their transport through any country prior to delivery.

A3   Contracts of carriage and insurance

(a) Contract of carriage

The seller must contract at its own expense for the carriage of the goods to the named place of destination or to the agreed point, if any, at the named place of destination. If a specific point is not agreed or is not determined by practice, the seller may select the point at the named place of destination that best suits its purpose.

(b) Contract of insurance

The seller has no obligation to the buyer to make a contract of insurance. However, the seller must provide the buyer, at the buyer's request, risk, and expense (if any), with information that the buyer needs for obtaining insurance.

A4   Delivery

The seller must deliver the goods by placing them at the disposal of the buyer on the arriving means of transport ready for unloading at the agreed point, if any, at the named place of destination on the agreed date or within the agreed period.

B THE BUYER'S OBLIGATIONS

B1 General obligations of the buyer

The buyer must pay the price of the goods as provided in the contract of sale.

Any document referred to in B1-B10 may be an equivalent electronic record or procedure if agreed between the parties or customary.

B2 Licenses, authorizations, security clearances and other formalities

Where applicable, the buyer must obtain, at its own risk and expense, any import licence or other official authorization and carry out all customs formalities for the import of the goods.

B3 Contracts of carriage and insurance

(a) Contract of carriage

The buyer has no obligation to the seller to make a contract of carriage.

(b) Contract of insurance

The buyer has no obligation to the seller to make a contract of insurance. However, the buyer must provide the seller, upon request, with the necessary information for obtaining insurance.

B4 Taking delivery

The buyer must take delivery of the goods when they have been delivered as envisaged in A4.

A5 Transfer of risks

The seller bears all risks of loss of or damage to the goods until they have been delivered in accordance with A4, with the exception of loss or damage in the circumstances described in B5.

A6 Allocation of costs

The seller must pay

(a) In addition to costs resulting from A3 (a), all costs relating to the goods until they have been delivered in accordance with A4, other than those payable by the buyer as envisaged in B6;

(b) Any charges for unloading at the place of destination that were for the seller's account under the contract of carriage; and

(c) Where applicable, the costs of customs formalities necessary for export as well as all duties, taxes and other charges payable upon export and the costs for their transport through any country, prior to delivery in accordance with A4.

A7   Notices to the buyer

The seller must give the buyer any notice needed in order to allow the buyer to take measures that are normally necessary to enable the buyer to take delivery of the goods.

A8   Delivery document

The seller must provide the buyer, at the seller's expense, with a document enabling the buyer to take delivery of the goods as envisaged in A4/B4.

B5   Transfer of risks

The buyer bears all risks of loss of or damage to the goods from the time they have been delivered as envisaged in A4. If

(a) The buyer fails to fulfill its obligations in accordance with B2, then it bears all resulting risks of loss of or damage to the goods; or

(b) The buyer fails to give notice in accordance with B7, then it bears all risks of loss of or damage to the goods from the agreed date or the expiry date of the agreed period for delivery, provided that the goods have been clearly identified as the contract goods.

B6   Allocation of costs

The buyer must pay

(a) All costs relating to the goods from the time they have been delivered as envisaged in A4;

(b) All costs of unloading necessary to take delivery of the goods from the arriving means of transport at the named place of destination, unless such costs were for the seller's account under the contract of carriage;

(c) Any additional costs incurred by the seller if the buyer fails to fulfill its obligations in accordance with B2 or to give notice in accordance with B7, provided that the goods have been clearly identified as the contract goods; and

(d) Where applicable, the costs of customs formalities, as well as all duties, taxes and other charges payable upon import of the goods.

B7　Notices to the seller

The buyer must, whenever it is entitled to determine the time within an agreed period and/or the point of taking delivery within the named place of destination, give the seller sufficient notice thereof.

B8　Proof of delivery

The buyer must accept the delivery document provided as envisaged in A8.

A9　Checking-packaging-marking

The seller must pay the costs of those checking operations (such as checking quality, measuring, weighing, counting) that are necessary for the purpose of delivering the goods in accordance with A4, as well as the costs of any pre-shipment inspection mandated by the authority of the country of export. The seller must, at its own expense, package the goods, unless it is usual for the particular trade to transport the type of goods sold unpackaged. The seller may package the goods in the manner appropriate for their transport, unless the buyer has notified the seller of specific packaging requirements before the contract of sale is concluded. Packaging is to be marked appropriately.

A10　Assistance with information and related costs

The seller must, where applicable, in a timely manner, provide to or render assistance in obtaining for the buyer, at the buyer's request, risk and expense, any documents and information, including security-related information, that the buyer needs for the import of the goods and/or for their transport to the final destination. The seller must reimburse the buyer for all costs and charges incurred by the buyer in providing or rendering assistance in obtaining documents and information as envisaged in B10.

B9　Inspection of goods

The buyer must pay the costs of any mandatory pre-shipment inspection, except when such inspection is mandated by the authorities of the country of export.

B10 Assistance with information and related costs

The buyer must, in a timely manner, advise the seller of any security information requirements so that the seller may comply with A10. The buyer must reimburse the seller for all costs and charges incurred by the seller in providing or rendering assistance in obtaining documents and information as envisaged in A10.

The buyer must, where applicable, in a timely manner, provide to or render assistance in obtaining for the seller, at the seller's request, risk and expense, any documents and information, including security-related information, that the seller needs for the transport and export of the goods and for their transport through any country.

It should be noted that DAT and DAP are two new terms under Incoterms 2010. Actually DAT replaces DEQ under Incoterms 2000, while DAP replaces DAF, DES and DDU under Incoterms 2000.

What is the difference between DAT and DAP?

5.2.7 DDP (DELIVERED DUTY PAID) (insert named place of destination) Incoterms 2010

This rule may be used irrespective of the mode of transport selected and may also be used where more than one mode of transport is employed. "Delivered Duty Paid" means that the seller delivers the goods when the goods are placed at the disposal of the buyer, cleared for import on the arriving means of transport ready for unloading at the named place of destination. The seller bears all the costs and risks involved in bringing the goods to the place of destination and has an obligation to clear the goods not only for export but also for import, to pay any duty for both export and import and to carry out all customs formalities.

DDP represents the maximum obligation for the seller. The parties are well advised to specify as clearly as possible the point within the agreed place of destination, as the costs and risks to that point are for the account of the seller. The seller is advised to procure contracts of carriage that match this choice precisely. If the seller incurs costs under its contract of carriage related to unloading at the place of destination, the seller is not entitled to recover such costs from the buyer unless otherwise agreed between the parties.

The parties are well advised not to use DDP if the seller is unable directly or indirectly to obtain import clearance. If the parties wish the buyer to bear all risks and costs of import clearance, the DAP rule should be used. Any VAT or other taxes payable upon import are for the seller's account unless expressly agreed otherwise in the sales contract.

5.3 Terms for Sea and Inland Waterway Transport

5.3.1 FAS (FREE ALONGSIDE SHIP)(insert named port of shipment) Incoterms 2010

This rule is to be used only for sea or inland waterway transport.

"Free Alongside Ship" means that the seller delivers when the goods are placed alongside the vessel (e.g., on a quay or a barge) nominated by the buyer at the named port of shipment. The risk of loss of or damage to the goods passes when the goods are alongside the ship, and the buyer bears all costs from that moment onwards. The parties are well advised to specify as clearly as possible the loading point at the named port of shipment, as the costs and risks to that point are for the account of the seller and these costs and associated handling charges may vary according to the practice of the port. The seller is required either to deliver the goods alongside the ship or to procure goods already so delivered for shipment. The reference to "procure" here caters for multiple sales down a chain ('string sales'), particularly common in the commodity trades.

Where the goods are in containers, it is typical for the seller to hand the goods over to the carrier at a terminal and not alongside the vessel. In such situations, the FAS rule would be inappropriate, and the FCA rule should be used. FAS requires the seller to clear the goods for export, where applicable. However, the seller has no obligation to clear the goods for import, pay any import duty or carry out any import customs formalities.

5.3.2 FOB (FREE ON BOARD) (insert named port of shipment) Incoterms 2010

This rule is to be used only for sea or inland waterway transport.

"Free on Board" means that the seller delivers the goods on board the vessel nominated by the buyer at the named port of shipment or procures the goods already so delivered. The risk of loss of or damage to the goods passes when the goods are on board the vessel, and the buyer bears all costs from that moment onwards.

The seller is required either to deliver the goods on board the vessel or to procure goods already so delivered for shipment. The reference to "procure" here caters for multiple sales down a chain ('string sales'), particularly common in the commodity trades.

FOB may not be appropriate where goods are handed over to the carrier before they are on board the vessel, for example goods in containers, which are typically delivered at a terminal. In such situations, the FCA rule should be used.

FOB requires the seller to clear the goods for export, where applicable. However, the seller has no obligation to clear the goods for import, pay any import duty or carry out any import customs formalities.

A THE SELLER'S OBLIGATIONS

A1 General obligations of the seller

The seller must provide the goods and the commercial invoice in conformity with the contract of sale and any other evidence of conformity that may be required by the contract. Any document referred to in A1-A10 may be an equivalent electronic record or procedure if agreed between the parties or customary.

A2 Licenses, authorizations, security clearances and other formalities

Where applicable, the seller must obtain, at its own risk and expense, any export license or other official authorization and carry out all customs formalities necessary for the export of the goods.

A3 Contracts of carriage and insurance
(a) Contract of carriage
The seller has no obligation to the buyer to make a contract of carriage. However, if requested by the buyer or if it is commercial practice and the buyer does not give an instruction to the contrary in due time, the seller may contract for carriage on usual terms at the buyer's risk and expense. In either case, the seller may decline to make the contract of carriage and, if it does, shall promptly notify the buyer.
(b) Contract of insurance
The seller has no obligation to the buyer to make a contract of insurance. However, the seller must provide the buyer, at the buyer's request, risk, and expense (if any), with information that the buyer needs for obtaining insurance.

A4 Delivery
The seller must deliver the goods either by placing them on board the vessel nominated by the buyer at the loading point, if any, indicated by the buyer at the named port of shipment or by procuring the goods so delivered. In either case, the seller must deliver the goods on the agreed date or within the agreed period and in the manner customary at the port. If no specific loading point has been indicated by the buyer, the seller may select the point within the named port of shipment that best suits its purpose.

B THE BUYER'S OBLIGATIONS
B1 General obligations of the buyer
The buyer must pay the price of the goods as provided in the contract of sale. Any document referred to in B1 – B10 may be an equivalent electronic record or procedure if agreed between the parties or customary.

B2 Licenses, authorizations, security clearances and other formalities
Where applicable, it is up to the buyer to obtain, at its own risk and expense, any import license or other official authorization and carry out all

customs formalities for the import of the goods and for their transport through any country.

B3　Contracts of carriage and insurance
(a) Contract of carriage
The buyer must contract, at its own expense for the carriage of the goods from the named port of shipment, except where the contract of carriage is made by the seller as provided for in A3 (a).
(b) Contract of insurance
The buyer has no obligation to the seller to make a contract of insurance.

B4　Taking delivery
The buyer must take delivery of the goods when they have been delivered as envisaged in A4.

A5　Transfer of risks
The seller bears all risks of loss of or damage to the goods until they have been delivered in accordance with A4 with the exception of loss or damage in the circumstances described in B5.

A6　Allocation of costs
The seller must pay:
(a) All costs relating to the goods until they have been delivered in accordance with A4, other than those payable by the buyer as envisaged in B6; and
(b) Where applicable, the costs of customs formalities necessary for export, as well as all duties, taxes and other charges payable upon export.

B5　Transfer of risks
The buyer bears all risks of loss of or damage to the goods from the time they have been delivered as envisaged in A4. If
(a) The buyer fails to notify the nomination of a vessel in accordance with B7; or

(b) The vessel nominated by the buyer fails to arrive on time to enable the seller to comply with A4, is unable to take the goods, or closes for cargo earlier than the time notified in accordance with B7; then, the buyer bears all risks of loss of or damage to the goods:

—from the agreed date, or in the absence of an agreed date,

—from the date notified by the seller under A7 within the agreed period, or, if no such date has been notified,

—from the expiry date of any agreed period for delivery, provided that the goods have been clearly identified as the contract goods.

B6　Allocation of costs

The buyer must pay:

(a) All costs relating to the goods from the time they have been delivered as envisaged in A4, except, where applicable, the costs of customs formalities necessary for export, as well as all duties, taxes and other charges payable upon export as referred to in A6 (b);

(b) any additional costs incurred, either because:

—the buyer has failed to give appropriate notice in accordance with B7, or

—the vessel nominated by the buyer fails to arrive on time, is unable to take the goods, or closes for cargo earlier than the time notified in accordance with B7, provided that the goods have been clearly identified as the contract goods; and

—where applicable, all duties, taxes and other charges, as well as the costs of carrying out customs formalities payable upon import of the goods and the costs for their transport through any country.

A7　Notices to the buyer

The seller must, at the buyer's risk and expense, give the buyer sufficient notice either that the goods have been delivered in accordance with A4 or that the vessel has failed to take the goods within the time agreed.

A8　Delivery document

The seller must provide the buyer, at the seller's expense, with the usual proof that the goods have been delivered in accordance with A4.

Unless such proof is a transport document, the seller must provide assistance to the buyer, at the buyer's request, risk and expense, in obtaining a transport document.

A9   Checking – packaging – marking

The seller must pay the costs of those checking operations (such as checking quality, measuring, weighing, counting) that are necessary for the purpose of delivering the goods in accordance with A4, as well as the costs of any pre-shipment inspection mandated by the authority of the country of export. The seller must, at its own expense, package the goods, unless it is usual for the particular trade to transport the type of goods sold unpackaged. The seller may package the goods in the manner appropriate for their transport, unless the buyer has notified the seller of specific packaging requirements before the contract of sale is concluded. Packaging is to be marked appropriately.

A10   Assistance with information and related costs

The seller must, where applicable, in a timely manner, provide to or render assistance in obtaining for the buyer, at the buyer's request, risk and expense, any documents and information, including security-related information, that the buyer needs for the import of the goods and/or for their transport to the final destination.

The seller must reimburse the buyer for all costs and charges incurred by the buyer in providing or rendering assistance in obtaining documents and information as envisaged in B10.

B7   Notices to the seller

The buyer must give the seller sufficient notice of the vessel name, loading point and, where necessary, the selected delivery time within the agreed period.

B8 Proof of delivery

The buyer must accept the proof of delivery provided as envisaged in A8.

B9 Inspection of goods

The buyer must pay the costs of any mandatory pre-shipment inspection, except when such inspection is mandated by the authorities of the country of export.

B10 Assistance with information and related costs

The buyer must, in a timely manner, advise the seller of any security information requirements so that the seller may comply with A10.

The buyer must reimburse the seller for all costs and charges incurred by the seller in providing or rendering assistance in obtaining documents and information as envisaged in A10.

The buyer must, where applicable, in a timely manner, provide to or render assistance in obtaining for the seller, at the seller's request, risk and expense, any documents and information, including security-related information, that the seller needs for the transport and export of the goods and for their transport through any country.

Case study:

中国某外贸公司以 FOB 价格条件出口棉纱 2000 包,每包净重 200 公斤。装船时已经双方认可的检验机构检验,货物符合合同规定的品质条件。该外贸公司装船后因疏忽未及时通知买方,直至 3 天后才给予装船通知。但在启航 18 小时后,船只遇风浪致使棉纱全部浸湿。买方因接到装船通知晚,未能及时办理保险手续,无法向保险公司索赔。买方要求卖方赔偿损失,卖方拒绝。发生争议。

问题:该合同中,货物风险是否已转移给买方?应如何处理?

FOB 条件下卖方的交货义务有两项:一是将货物装上船;二是装船之后必须及时向买方发出装船通知。而通知义务往往被忽视,如果卖方没有及时通知买方,即构成违约。

5.3.3　CFR(COST AND FREIGHT) (insert named port of destination) Incoterms 2010

This rule is to be used only for sea or inland waterway transport. "Cost and Freight" means that the seller delivers the goods on board the vessel or procures the goods already so delivered. The risk of loss of or damage to the goods passes when the goods are on board the vessel.

The seller must contract for and pay the costs and freight necessary to bring the goods to the named port of destination. When CPT, CIP, CFR or CIF are used, the seller fulfills its obligation to deliver when it hands the goods over to the carrier in the manner specified in the chosen rule and not when the goods reach the place of destination.

This rule has two critical points, because risk passes and costs are transferred at different places. While the contract will always specify a destination port, it might not specify the port of shipment, which is where risk passes to the buyer. If the shipment port is of particular interest to the buyer, the parties are well advised to identify it as precisely as possible in the contract.

The parties are well advised to identify as precisely as possible the point at the agreed port of destination, as the costs to that point are for the account of the seller. The seller is advised to procure contracts of carriage that match this choice precisely. If the seller incurs costs under its contract of carriage related to unloading at the specified point at the port of destination, the seller is not entitled to recover such costs from the buyer unless otherwise agreed between the parties. The seller is required either to deliver the goods on board the vessel or to procure goods already so delivered for shipment to the destination.

In addition, the seller is required either to make a contract of carriage or to procure such a contract. The reference to "procure" here caters for multiple sales down a chain ('string sales'), particularly common in the commodity trades.

CFR may not be appropriate where goods are handed over to the carrier before they are on board the vessel, for example goods in containers, which are typically delivered at a terminal. In such circumstances, the CPT rule should be used.

CFR requires the seller to clear the goods for export, where applicable. However, the seller has no obligation to clear the goods for import, pay any import duty or carry out any import customs formalities.

A THE SELLER'S OBLIGATIONS

A1　General obligations of the seller

The seller must provide the goods and the commercial invoice in conformity with the contract of sale and any other evidence of conformity that may be required by the contract. Any document referred to in A1-A10 may be an equivalent electronic record or procedure if agreed between the parties or customary.

A2　Licenses, authorizations, security clearances and other formalities

Where applicable, the seller must obtain, at its own risk and expense, any export license or other official authorization and carry out all customs formalities necessary for the export of the goods.

A3　Contracts of carriage and insurance

(a) Contract of carriage

The seller must contract or procure a contract for the carriage of the goods from the agreed point of delivery, if any, at the place of delivery to the named port of destination or, if agreed, any point at that port. The contract of carriage must be made on usual terms at the seller's expense and provide for carriage by the usual route in a vessel of the type normally used for the transport of the type of goods sold.

(b) Contract of insurance

The seller has no obligation to the buyer to make a contract of insurance. However, the seller must provide the buyer, at the buyer's request, risk, and expense (if any), with information that the buyer needs for obtaining insurance.

A4　Delivery

The seller must deliver the goods either by placing them on board the vessel or by procuring the goods so delivered. In either case, the seller must deliver the goods on the agreed date or within the agreed period and in the manner customary at the port.

B THE BUYER'S OBLIGATIONS

B1 General obligations of the buyer

The buyer must pay the price of the goods as provided in the contract of sale. Any document referred to in B1-B10 may be an equivalent electronic record or procedure if agreed between the parties or customary.

B2 Licenses, authorizations, security clearances and other formalities

Where applicable, it is up to the buyer to obtain, at its own risk and expense, any import license or other official authorization and carry out all customs formalities for the import of the goods and for their transport through any country.

B3 Contracts of carriage and insurance

(a) Contract of carriage

The buyer has no obligation to the seller to make a contract of carriage.

(b) Contract of insurance

The buyer has no obligation to the seller to make a contract of insurance. However, the buyer must provide the seller, upon request, with the necessary information for obtaining insurance.

B4 Taking delivery

The buyer must take delivery of the goods when they have been delivered as envisaged in A4 and receive them from the carrier at the named port of destination.

A5 Transfer of risks

The seller bears all risks of loss of or damage to the goods until they have been delivered in accordance with A4, with the exception of loss or damage in the circumstances described in B5.

A6　Allocation of costs

The seller must pay

(a) All costs relating to the goods until they have been delivered in accordance with A4, other than those payable by the buyer as envisaged in B6;

(b) The freight and all other costs resulting from A3 (a), including the costs of loading the goods on board and any charges for unloading at the agreed port of discharge that were for the seller's account under the contract of carriage; and

(c) Where applicable, the costs of customs formalities necessary for export as well as all duties, taxes and other charges payable upon export, and the costs for their transport through any country that were for the seller's account under the contract of carriage.

A7　Notices to the buyer

The seller must give the buyer any notice needed in order to allow the buyer to take measures that are normally necessary to enable the buyer to take the goods.

B5　Transfer of risks

The buyer bears all risks of loss of or damage to the goods from the time they have been delivered as envisaged in A4. If the buyer fails to give notice in accordance with B7, then it bears all risks of loss of or damage to the goods from the agreed date or the expiry date of the agreed period for shipment, provided that the goods have been clearly identified as the contract goods.

B6　Allocation of costs

The buyer must, subject to the provisions of A3 (a), pay

(a) All costs relating to the goods from the time they have been delivered as envisaged in A4, except, where applicable, the costs of customs formalities necessary for export as well as all duties, taxes, and other charges payable upon export as referred to in A6 (c);

(b) All costs and charges relating to the goods while in transit until their arrival at the port of destination, unless such costs and charges were for the seller's account under the contract of carriage;

(c) Unloading costs including lighterage and wharfage charges, unless such costs and charges were for the seller's account under the contract of carriage;

(d) Any additional costs incurred if it fails to give notice in accordance with B7, from the agreed date or the expiry date of the agreed period for shipment, provided that the goods have been clearly identified as the contract goods; and

(e) Where applicable, all duties, taxes and other charges, as well as the costs of carrying out customs formalities payable upon import of the goods and the costs for their transport through any country unless included within the cost of the contract of carriage.

B7   Notices to the seller

The buyer must, whenever it is entitled to determine the time for shipping the goods and/or the point of receiving the goods within the named port of destination, give the seller sufficient notice thereof.

A8   Delivery document

The seller must, at its own expense, provide the buyer without delay with the usual transport document for the agreed port of destination. This transport document must cover the contract goods, be dated within the period agreed for shipment, enable the buyer to claim the goods from the carrier at the port of destination and, unless otherwise agreed, enable the buyer to sell the goods in transit by the transfer of the document to a subsequent buyer or by notification to the carrier. When such a transport document is issued in negotiable form and in several originals, a full set of originals must be presented to the buyer.

A9   Checking – packaging – marking

The seller must pay the costs of those checking operations (such as checking quality, measuring, weighing, counting) that are necessary for the purpose of delivering the goods in accordance with A4, as well as the costs of any pre-shipment inspection mandated by the authority of the country of export. The seller must, at its own expense, package the goods, unless it is usual for the particular trade to transport the type of goods sold unpackaged. The seller may package the goods in the manner appropriate for their transport, unless the buyer has notified the seller of specific packaging requirements before the contract of sale is concluded. Packaging is to be marked appropriately.

A10　Assistance with information and related costs

The seller must, where applicable, in a timely manner, provide to or render assistance in obtaining for the buyer, at the buyer's request, risk and expense, any documents and information, including security-related information, that the buyer needs for the import of the goods and/or for their transport to the final destination.

The seller must reimburse the buyer for all costs and charges incurred by the buyer in providing or rendering assistance in obtaining documents and information as envisaged in B10.

B8　Proof of delivery

The buyer must accept the transport document provided as envisaged in A8 if it is in conformity with the contract.

B9　Inspection of goods

The buyer must pay the costs of any mandatory pre-shipment inspection, except when such inspection is mandated by the authorities of the country of export.

B10　Assistance with information and related costs

The buyer must, in a timely manner, advise the seller of any security information requirements so that the seller may comply with A10.

The buyer must reimburse the seller for all costs and charges incurred by the seller in providing or rendering assistance in obtaining documents and information as envisaged in A10.

The buyer must, where applicable, in a timely manner, provide to or render assistance in obtaining for the seller, at the seller's request, risk and expense, any documents and information, including security-related information, that the seller needs for the transport and export of the goods and for their transport through any country.

5.3.4 CIF (COST INSURANCE AND FREIGHT) (insert named port of destination) Incoterms 2010

This rule is to be used only for sea or inland waterway transport.

"Cost, Insurance and Freight" means that the seller delivers the goods on board the vessel or procures the goods already so delivered. The risk of loss of or damage to the goods passes when the goods are on board the vessel. The seller must contract for and pay the costs and freight necessary to bring the goods to the named port of destination.

The seller also contracts for insurance cover against the buyer's risk of loss of or damage to the goods during the carriage. The buyer should note that under CIF the seller is required to obtain insurance only on minimum cover. Should the buyer wish to have more insurance protection, it will need either to agree as much expressly with the seller or to make its own extra insurance arrangements.

When CPT, CIP, CFR, or CIF are used, the seller fulfills its obligation to deliver when it hands the goods over to the carrier in the manner specified in the chosen rule and not when the goods don't reach the place of destination.

This rule has two critical points, because risk passes and costs are transferred at different places. While the contract will always specify a destination port, it might not specify the port of shipment, which is where risk passes to the buyer. If the shipment port is of particular interest to the buyer, the parties are well advised to identify it as precisely as possible in the contract.

The parties are well advised to identify as precisely as possible the point at the agreed port of destination, as the costs to that point are for the account of the seller. The seller is advised to procure contracts of carriage that match this choice precisely. If the seller incurs costs under its contract of carriage related to unloading at the specified point at the port of destination, the seller is not entitled to recover such costs from the buyer unless otherwise agreed between the parties.

The seller is required either to deliver the goods on board the vessel or to procure goods already so delivered for shipment to the destination. In addition, the seller is required either to make a contract of carriage or to procure such a contract. The reference to "procure" here caters for multiple sales down a chain ('string sales'), particularly common in the commodity trades.

CIF may not be appropriate where goods are handed over to the carrier before they are on board the vessel, for example goods in containers, which are typically delivered at a terminal. In such circumstances, the CIP rule should be used. CIF requires the seller to clear the goods for export, where applicable. However, the seller has no obligation to clear the goods for import, pay any import duty or carry out any import customs formalities.

A   THE SELLER'S OBLIGATIONS

A1   General obligations of the seller

The seller must provide the goods and the commercial invoice in conformity with the contract of sale and any other evidence of conformity that may be required by the contract. Any document referred to in A1-A10 may be an equivalent electronic record or procedure if agreed between the parties or customary.

A2   Licenses, authorizations, security clearances and other formalities

Where applicable, the seller must obtain, at its own risk and expense, any export license or other official authorization and carry out all customs formalities necessary for the export of the goods.

B   THE BUYER'S OBLIGATIONS

B1   General obligations of the buyer

The buyer must pay the price of the goods as provided in the contract of sale. Any document referred to in B1-B10 may be an equivalent electronic record or procedure if agreed between the parties or customary.

B2   Licenses, authorizations, security clearances and formalities

Where applicable, it is up to the buyer to obtain, at its own risk and expense, any import license or other official authorization and carry out all customs formalities for the import of the goods and for their transport through any country.

A3   Contracts of carriage and insurance

(a) Contract of carriage

The seller must contract or procure a contract for the carriage of the goods from the agreed point of delivery, if any, at the place of delivery to the named port of destination or, if agreed, any point at that port. The contract of carriage must be made on usual terms at the seller's expense and provide for carriage by the usual route in a vessel of the type normally used for the transport of the type of goods sold.

(b) Contract of insurance

The seller must obtain, at its own expense, cargo insurance complying at least with the minimum cover provided by Clauses (c) of the Institute Cargo Clauses (LMA/IUA) or any similar clauses. The insurance shall be contracted with underwriters or an insurance company of good repute and entitle the buyer, or any other person having an insurable interest in the goods, to claim directly from the insurer.

When required by the buyer, the seller shall, subject to the buyer providing any necessary information requested by the seller, provide at the buyer's expense any additional cover, if procurable, such as cover as provided by Clauses (a) or (b) of the Institute Cargo Clauses (LMA/IUA) or any similar clauses and/or cover complying with the Institute War Clauses and/or Institute Strikes Clauses (LMA/IUA) or any similar clauses. The insurance shall cover, at a minimum, the price provided in the contract plus 10% (i.e., 110%) and shall be in the currency of the contract. The insurance shall cover the goods from the point of delivery set out in A4 and A5 to at least the named port of destination. The seller must provide the buyer with the insurance policy or other evidence of insurance cover. Moreover, the seller must provide the buyer, at the buyer's request, risk, and expense (if any), with information that the buyer needs to procure any additional insurance.

A4 Delivery

The seller must deliver the goods either by placing them on board the vessel or by procuring the goods so delivered. In either case, the seller must deliver the goods on the agreed date or within the agreed period and in the manner customary at the port.

B3 Contracts of carriage and insurance

(a) Contract of carriage

The buyer has no obligation to the seller to make a contract of carriage.

(b) Contract of insurance

The buyer has no obligation to the seller to make a contract of insurance. However, the buyer must provide the seller, upon request, with any information necessary for the seller to procure any additional insurance requested by the buyer as envisaged in A3 (b).

B4 Taking delivery

The buyer must take delivery of the goods when they have been delivered as envisaged in A4 and receive them from the carrier at the named port of destination.

A5 Transfer of risks

The seller bears all risks of loss of or damage to the goods until they have been delivered in accordance with A4, with the exception of loss or damage in the circumstances described in B5.

A6 Allocation of costs

The seller must pay

(a) All costs relating to the goods until they have been delivered in accordance with A4, other than those payable by the buyer as envisaged in B6;

(b) The freight and all other costs resulting from A3 (a), including the costs of loading the goods on board and any charges for unloading at the agreed port of discharge that were for the seller's account under the contract of carriage;

(c) The costs of insurance resulting from A3 (b); and

(d) Where applicable, the costs of customs formalities necessary for export, as well as all duties, taxes and other charges payable upon export, and the costs for their transport through any country that were for the seller's account under the contract of carriage.

B5 Transfer of risks

The buyer bears all risks of loss of or damage to the goods from the time they have been delivered as envisaged in A4. If the buyer fails to give notice in accordance with B7, then it bears all risks of loss of or damage to the goods from the agreed date or the expiry date of the agreed period for shipment, provided that the goods have been clearly identified as the contract goods.

B6 Allocation of costs

The buyer must, subject to the provisions of A3 (a), pay

(a) All costs relating to the goods from the time they have been delivered as envisaged in A4, except, where applicable, the costs of customs formalities necessary for export, as well as all duties, taxes and other charges payable upon export as referred to in A6 (d);

(b) All costs and charges relating to the goods while in transit until their arrival at the port of destination, unless such costs and charges were for the seller's account under the contract of carriage;

(c) Unloading costs including lighterage and wharfage charges, unless such costs and charges were for the seller's account under the contract of carriage;

(d) Any additional costs incurred if it fails to give notice in accordance with B7, from the agreed date or the expiry date of the agreed period for shipment, provided that the goods have been clearly identified as the contract goods;

(e) Where applicable, all duties, taxes and other charges, as well as the costs of carrying out customs formalities payable upon import of the goods and the costs for their transport through any country, unless included within the cost of the contract of carriage; and

(f) The costs of any additional insurance procured at the buyer's request under A3 (b) and B3 (b).

A7 Notices to the buyer

The seller must give the buyer any notice needed in order to allow the buyer to take measures that are normally necessary to enable the buyer to take the goods.

A8 Delivery document

The seller must, at its own expense provide the buyer without delay with the usual transport document for the agreed port of destination. This transport document must cover the contract goods, be dated within the period agreed for shipment, enable the buyer to claim the goods from the carrier at the port of destination and, unless otherwise agreed, enable the buyer to sell the goods in transit by the transfer of the document to a subsequent buyer or by notification to the carrier. When such a transport document is issued in negotiable form and in several originals, a full set of originals must be presented to the buyer.

A9　Checking – packaging – marking

The seller must pay the costs of those checking operations (such as checking quality, measuring, weighing, counting) that are necessary for the purpose of delivering the goods in accordance with A4, as well as the costs of any pre-shipment inspection mandated by the authority of the country of export.

The seller must, at its own expense, package the goods, unless it is usual for the particular trade to transport the type of goods sold unpackaged. The seller may package the goods in the manner appropriate for their transport, unlessthe buyer has notified the seller of specific packaging requirements before the contract of sale is concluded. Packaging is to be marked appropriately.

B7　Notices to the seller

The buyer must, whenever it is entitled to determine the time for shipping the goods and/or the point of receiving the goods within the named port of destination, give the seller sufficient notice thereof.

B8　Proof of delivery

The buyer must accept the transport document provided as envisaged in A8 if it is in conformity with the contract.

B9　Inspection of goods

The buyer must pay the costs of any mandatory pre-shipment inspection, except when such inspection is mandated by the authorities of the country of export.

A10　Assistance with information and related costs

The seller must, where applicable, in a timely manner, provide to or render assistance in obtaining for the buyer, at the buyer's request, risk and expense, any documents and information, including security-related information, that the buyer needs for the import of the goods and/or for their transport to the final destination.

The seller must reimburse the buyer for all costs and charges incurred by the buyer in providing or rendering assistance in obtaining documents and information as envisaged in B10.

B10   Assistance with information and related costs

The buyer must, in a timely manner, advise the seller of any security information requirements so that the seller may comply with A10.

The buyer must reimburse the seller for all costs and charges incurred by the seller in providing or rendering assistance in obtaining documents and information as envisaged in A10.

The buyer must, where applicable, in a timely manner, provide to or render assistance in obtaining for the seller, at the seller's request, risk and expense, any documents and information, including security-related information, that the seller needs for the transport and export of the goods and for their transport through any country.

Case study：

某出口公司按CIF伦敦向英商出售一批核桃仁，由于该商品季节性较强，双方在合同中规定：买方须于9月底前将信用证开到，卖方保证运货船只不迟于12月2日驶抵目的港。如货轮迟于12月2日抵达目的港，买方有权取消合同，如货款已收，卖方必须将货款退还买方。问这一份合同的性质是否属于CIF合同？

5.4   Calculation of Quotation

e.g. USD 100 per cozen CIF C 2% New York
Price including commission＝net price/(1－commission rate)

e.g. CIF 200美元，佣金率5%，则：
　　　　含佣价＝200/(1－5%)＝210.526(美元)
　　　　佣金＝210.526×5%＝10.526(美元)

e.g. 单价:每公吨 335 美元 CIF 纽约包含佣金 2%,合同成立后,不得调整价格。

No price adjustment shall be allowed after conclusion of this contract.

(1)在收到对方的询盘函后,正昌贸易有限公司进行报价核算,并根据对方要求,寄去灯具样品。

报价核算资料:

商品 6 个型号共订购 140 000 只,其中以 40 瓦透明灯具(Candle lamps E27 cap 230/240V 40W transparent)为例进行报价核算。本次对方订购的商品数量合计装一个 20 英尺集装箱。

报价数量:20 000 只。

进货价格:1.17 元(含 17%增值税),同时灯具商品的出口退税率为 17%。

国内费用:预计本批货物(包括其他型号)即 140 000 只灯具国内运杂费共计 1600 元,商检报关费共计 800 元,港区港杂费共计 600 元,其他费用共计 1200 元。

海洋运费:从上海至加拿大多伦多一个 20 英尺集装箱 1800 美元。

货运保险:按 CIF C3%价格的 110%投保一切险和战争险,保险费率为0.6%、0.03%,且灯具指明货物保险加保费 2%。

客户佣金:成交价格的 3%。

报价利润:按报价的 20%。

报价汇率:8.27 元人民币兑换 1 美元。

报出 CIF C3%多伦多美元单价。

解:

进货成本=1.17÷(1+17%)÷8.27=0.121(美元)

国内费用=(1600+800+600+1200)÷140000÷8.27=0.0036(美元)

运费=1800÷140000=0.0129(美元)

保险费=CIF C3%×110%×(0.6%+0.03%+2%)
     =0.02893 CIF C3%价

客户佣金=CIF C3%价×3%

利润=CIF C3%×20%

CIF C3%价=0.121+0.0036+0.0129+(0.02893+0.03+0.2)
          ×CIF C3%价

$$\text{CIF C3\%价} = \frac{0.121+0.0036+0.0129}{1-0.02893-0.03-0.2} = 0.186(美元)$$

(2) 祥瑞进出口公司欲出口 1000 台货号为 XY-3H 的电脑检测仪至马来西亚。电脑检测仪的购货成本为 1980 元,包含 17% 的增值税。已知电脑检测仪的出口退税率为 9%。国内运杂费共计 2500 元,商检报关费共 900 元,其他费用共计 800 元,公司预期利润为 9%(按报价的 9%),对方公司要求的佣金为 3%。请报出 FOB C3% 的价格(美元汇率为 8.27∶1)。

解:实际成本:

$$1980 \times (1 - \frac{9\%}{1+17\%}) = 1827.69(元人民币)$$

国内费用:

$$(2500 + 900 + 800) \div 1000 = 4.2(元人民币)$$

FOB C3% 报价:

$$\frac{1827.69 + 4.2}{1 - 9\% - 3\%} = 2081.6931(元人民币) = 251.72(美元)$$

Exercise

I. *Multiple choice*

1. The two new terms under Incoterms 2010 are _____.
   A. DAF and DDP 　　　　　　B. DAT and DAP
   C. DES and DAF 　　　　　　D. DAT and DAF

2. Alterations to the following are considered material change of offer EXCEPT _____.
   A. number of copies of documents　　B. delivery time
   C. price terms　　　　　　　　　　　D. settlement of disputes

3. Under which term should the seller carry out import formalities?
   A. EXW　　　B. FCA　　　C. DDU　　　D. DDP

4. The difference between FOB and FAS lies in _____.
   A. loading　　B. transfer of risks　　C. unloading　　D. Freight

5. _____ can be used for all kinds of mode of transport.
   A. CIF　　　B. CFR　　　C. FOB　　　D. FCA.

6. Which term requires the seller to insure the goods against minimum coverage by the seller? (　　)
   A. CIF　　　B. FCA　　　C. FAS　　　D. FOB

7. The term CFR should be followed by _____.

    A. point of origin   B. port of destination
    C. port of shipment   D. port of exportation
8. The term CPT should be followed by _____.
    A. place of importation   B. port of shipment
    C. port of destination   D. place of exportation
9. Which isn't a negotiable document among the four in the following? _____
    A. bill of lading B. bill of exchange C. packing list D. insurance policy
10. Which term represents the maximum obligations for seller? _____
    A. EXW   B. DAF   C. DDP   D. CPT

Ⅱ. *True or false statements*

1. FAS 贸易术语与 FOB 术语在交货上的区别是 FAS 在船边交货,而 FOB 在船上交货。
2. 在 FCA 术语下,货物的风险在船舷转移。
3. 在 FOB 术语下,货物的风险在卸货港船舷转移。
4. FOB 和 FAS 贸易术语主要适用于海运或内河运输,而 FCA 则适用于各种运输方式。
5. 以 CIF 条件成交的合同,当货物在运输途中受损后,卖方有权凭符合合同规定的全套单据向买方索取货款,而且事后买方没有索赔权。
6. 在一般情况下,按 CFR 贸易术语成交的出口合同中,保险费不应计入货物价格。
7. 在下列条件成交的合同中:CIF 东京,FOB 上海,DES 雅加达,CFR 伦敦,只有 FOB 上海不属于装运合同。
8. 按照 CFR 条件成交的合同双方,风险与费用的划分点均在装运港船舷。

Ⅲ. *Questions*

1. What is the purpose of shipping advice?
2. What kind of transportation is FOB appropriate for?
3. What is the common feature among FCA, FAS, FOB?
4. What is the difference between FAS and FOB?

Ⅳ. *Case study*

1. A Company in Shanghai quotes its exporting price, USD 50.00 Per case CFR C3% Kuwait. But the foreign company requires the Shanghai exporter to offer FOB Shanghai net price. If the standard of calculating basic freight of the

exporting goods is "W/M"; the measurement of a case with goods is 42×28×25 cubic centimeters and it's gross weight is 0.2 Metric Ton, the basic freight rate for the goods is USD 70.00 per freight ton.

  Please calculate how much this exporting company should offer FOB Shanghai price per case with the same profit.

2. 我出口公司对日商报出大豆实盘，每公吨 CIF 大阪 150 美元，发货港口是大连，现日商要求我方改报 FOB 大连价，我出口公司对价格应如何调整？如果最后按 FOB 条件签订合同，买卖双方在所承担的责任、费用和风险方面有什么差别？

Chapter 6　Ocean Transport

Ocean transport
Shipment clause in contract
Bill of Lading

6.1　Ocean Transport

6.1.1　Liner transport

Merchant vessels are operated in two ways. The first type of merchant vessels is liners. A liner is a passenger or cargo vessel that operates over a regular route according to an advertised time-table. It has the following features:
- fixed route, ports, schedule and relatively fixed freight;
- loading and unloading expenses included in freight;
- simple procedures;
- proper for cargo of small quantity.

As the freight rate is relatively fixed, the liner is both responsible for loading goods onto the vessel and unloading goods from the vessel. Freight is collected in different ways.

6.1.2　Shipping by chartering

The other type of merchant vessels is charter shipping. Compared with liners, Charter shipping has following characteristics:
- no fixed route, ports, schedule but direct trip;

- ideal for bulk cargoes of low value and huge quantity like oil, coal, ore and grain;
- freight determined by market.

As the freight under charter shipping is not relatively fixed, one issue needs to be clarified as to who should bear the loading and unloading costs. Three key terms have been developed to specify the responsibilities of the parties in a trade transaction.

- Free in(FI)

FI means the charterer of a vessel(shipper) is responsible for the cost of loading goods onto the vessel.

- Free out(FO)

FO indicates that the charterer of a vessel (shipper) is responsible for unloading goods from the vessel.

- Free in and out(FIO)

FIO means that the charterer of a vessel(shipper) is responsible for the costs of loading goods onto the vessel and unloading goods from the vessel. As for most types of cargo, freight is collected by weight(W), by volume(M), or by weight or volume (W/M). For certain cargoes, freight is charged by the estimated value of the cargo(Ad Valorem, or AV). For huge quantity of cargo like grain, coal, ore, etc., freight rate is open to negotiation.

6.2　Shipment Clause in Contract

Shipment clause specifies all the details about the shipment of goods. The details include time of shipment, port of shipment and port of destination, shipping advice, partial shipment and transshipment, etc.

6.2.1　Time of shipment

There are basically three ways to stipulate the time of shipment.

(1) Stipulating the specific time.

e.g. Shipment during July; shipment not later than July 31st; shipment at or before the end of September.

(2) Creating a link between the time of shipment and deadline by which the relevant L/C must reach the seller.

Chapter 6 Ocean Transport

e. g. Shipment within 30 days after receipt of L/C.

(3) Immediate shipment; prompt shipment; shipment as soon as possible.

6.2.2 Port of shipment and port of destination

Port of shipment and port of destination can be specified when the contract is signed. If a decision cannot be made by that time, several alterations can be listed and a time limit can be set by which the seller or the buyer must notify the other party which port is to be the port of shipment or destination.

6.2.3 Partial shipment and transshipment

Partial shipment means shipping the commodity under one contract by more than one shipment. Transshipment means the cargo being shipped will change before reaching the port of destination. If the bill of lading incorporates clauses stating that the carrier reserves the right to transship, then the transshipment is allowed even if the L/C prohibits transshipment.

e. g. (1) Shipment during May, with partial shipment and transshipment allowed.

(2) During May in two shipments, transshipment is prohibited.

6.2.4 Shipping notice/ advice of shipment

Shipping advice is used to coordinate the responsibilities of the exporter and the importer. For example, shipping advice is necessary when FOB term is used. The exporter needs to know when the ship will arrive to pick up the goods so that he can get the goods prepared for delivery. On the other hand, the importer needs to know when the goods are loaded on board the vessel so that he can arrange insurance and when he should be ready to take delivery of goods.

6.3 Bill of Lading

Before we look at Bill of Lading, three questions should be considered:
Who issues the B/L?
Whom is the B/L issued to?
When is the B/L issued?

Sample of B/L:

① SHIPPER		⑩ B/L NO.
② CONSIGNEE		C O S C O 中国远洋运输(集团)总公司 CHINA OCEAN SHIPPING (GROUP) CO. ORIGINAL COMBINED TRANPORT BILL OF LADING
③ NOTIFY PARTY		
④ PLACE OF RECEIPT	⑤ OCEAN VESSEL	
⑥ VOYAGE NO	⑦ PORT OF LOADING	
⑧ PORT OF DISCHARGE	⑨ PLACE OF DELIVERY	

| ⑪ MARKS ⑫) NOS. & KINDS OF PKGS ⑬ DESCRIPTION OF GOODS |
| ⑭ G. W. (kg) ⑮ MEAS(m³) |
| |
| ⑯ TOTAL NUMBER OF CONTAINERS OR PACKAGES(IN WORDS) |

FREIGHT & CHARGES	REVENUE TONS	RATE	PER	PREPAID	COLLECT
PREPAID AT	PAYABLE AT		⑰ PLACE AND DATE OF ISSUE		
TOTAL PREPAID	⑱ NUMBER OF ORIGINAL B(S)L				
LOADING ON BOARD THE VESSEL ⑲ DATE			⑳ BY		

6.3.1 Contents in a B/L

shipper(托运人);consignee (收货人);
port of loading; port of destination;
vessel name; shipping marks; description of goods;
No. of packages; gross weight; measurement;
copies; freight; shipping company; date and place.

6.3.2 Functions of B/L

(1) It is a receipt for goods signed by the shipping company and given to the shippers. The Carrier is responsible for delivering the goods in good condition.

(2) It is evidence of a contract of carriage between the shipping company and shipper.

Can we consider Bill of Lading as a contract of carriage?

(3) It is a document of title because the legal owner of the B/L is the owner of the goods. So, if we put the buyer's name in the consignee, it means that only the buyer is the owner of goods. In this case, is it beneficial to the seller? If the buyer does not want to pay, the seller will suffer the loss. So, what should we put here in consignee? It depends on the types of B/L.

6.3.3 Classifications of B/L

6.3.3.1 Clean B/L and unclean B/L

(1) Clean B/L

When B/L stating the goods "in apparent good order and condition" and this statement is not modified by the shipowner, then the B/L is called "clean B/L".

(2) Unclean B/L or dirty B/L

When a B/L bears remarks such as " insufficiently packed" "wet by rain" "some bags torn" etc. , it is called "unclean B/L".

6.3.3.2 Straight B/L, Order B/L and bearer B/L

(1) Order B/L(指示提单)

An order B/L is one in which the goods are consigned to the order of a named party. The L/C usually requires an order B/L by using such words as "to order" or "to order of (the named party)". It is a negotiable bill of lading as the title to the goods is conferred to the order of shipper or to the order of a named party. Furthermore, it is transferable only by endorsement[①]. This type of B/L is used to protect the interests of the shipper or the named party in the title to the goods.

If a L/C calls for a B/L that is "to order blank endorsed", the consignee field in the B/L should be put "To Order". If a L/C requires a B/L that is "to order of shipper and blank endorsed", then put the words "To Order of (shipper's name)" in the consignee field. The blank endorsement does not have the name of the endorsee and makes the B/L a bearer B/L.

In addition to blank endorsement, an order B/L can also be made to order of shipper and endorsed to order of a named party, under which the endorsement is called special endorsement. In the above two cases, the B/L remains an order instrument and can be further transferred by that named party.

However, if restrictive endorsement is made to an order B/L, the B/L can no longer be transferred.

(2) Straight B/L

A straight B/L is one in which the goods are consigned to a designated party or the consignee of the B/L is specific. The L/C requires a straight B/L by using such words as "consigned to (the named party)" or "issued in the name of (the named party)". It is a non-transferable bill of lading as the title to the goods is conferred directly to a party name in the letter of credit and is not transferable to another party by endorsement. Therefore, the use of a straight bill of lading has a higher risk for the seller unless the cash payment has been received by the seller or the buyer's integrity is unquestionable.

---

①Endorsement: the placing of one's signature on the reverse of a commercial document primarily for the purpose of transferring the rights of the document holder to some other person.

(3) Bearer B/L

This type of B/L makes the consignee "to bearer" or leaves it blank. Therefore, no endorsement is needed to transfer the document and the delivery of the cargo shall be made to any bearer of the B/L. Such B/L has a high risk to both parties and is not much in use now.

If you are the buyer, which B/L do you prefer, Bearer B/L or Order B/L?

Case study:

If a letter of credit bears such remarks as:

FULL SET OF CLEAN ON BOARD OCEAN BILLS OF LADING, MARKED " FREIGHT PREPAID " NOTIFYING LIAONING OCEAN FISHING CO. , LTD. TEL:(86)411-3680288.

一整套清洁已装船提单,抬头为 TO ORDER 的空白背书,且注明运费已付,通知人为 LIAONING OCEAN FISHING CO. , LTD. TEL:(86)411-3680288.

How do we understand "MADE OUT TO ORDER AND BLANK ENDORSED"? Why is it so popular in L/C?

6.3.3.3 Shipped /On board B/L, Received for shipment B/L and on deck B/L

(1) Shipped /On board B/L

This B/L indicates that the goods have been shipped or loaded on a named vessel, as evidenced by the notation "on board" or "shipped on board" on the bill of loading. It is issued only when the cargo has been shipped or loaded on board the vessel.

(2) Received for shipment B/L

Unlike shipped /On board B/L, this B/L does not indicate that the goods have been shipped. It only acknowledges that the goods have been received by the carrier for shipment but not yet loaded on board a vessel. Therefore, it does not have the date of shipment and a name of vessel. This type of B/L is often used for the shipper to negotiate the B/L at an earliest possible date.

(3) On deck B/L

On deck B/L is issued when the cargo is not loaded into the ship's hold but place on the deck of the ship. Unless otherwise stipulated in the letter of credit, the bill of lading must not indicate that the goods are or will be loaded on deck because of the high risks the cargo has to face.

6.3.3.4 Ante-dated B/L and advanced B/L

An ante-dated B/L is issued when the actual date of loading is later than the date set in the contract or the letter of credit. It is used by some shippers when they are able to effect shipment in time. The issuing date of this B/L is earlier than the actual date of loading in order to meet the L/C requirements.

However, an advanced B/L is in fact issued before loading the cargo on board the ship in order to negotiate payment before L/C expires or to negotiate at an earliest possible date.

It is noted that for both ante-dated B/L and advanced B/L, the issuing date of B/L is not in accordance with the actual date of loading. Therefore, they can be interpreted as fraud.

6.3.4 Common discrepancies in B/L

As Bill of Lading represents the title to the goods, it must be handled in accordance with the letter of credit. Any discrepancy in this document may result in non-payment by the bank or the buyer. The common discrepancies found in B/L are as follows:

- Document not presented in full set as requested;
- Alterations not authenticated by shipping company or its agent;
- Unacceptable type of B/L, e.g., on deck, dirty, charter party, etc.;
- Not endorsed "on board" when required;
- B/L not blank endorsed;
- Failure to indicate if freight prepaid or freight collected;
- Inconsistency between B/L and other documents;
- Document dated later than the shipping date in L/C;
- Late presentation for negotiation-beyond the earlier date of the L/C date of expiry and the L/C date of presentation (maximum 21days after B/L issuance).

Chapter 6　Ocean Transport

UCP 600 - Article 19　Transport Document Covering at Least Two Different Modes of Transport

a. A transport document covering at least two different modes of transport (multimodal or combined transport document), however named, must appear to:

i. indicate the name of the carrier and be signed by:

—the carrier or a named agent for or on behalf of the carrier, or

—the master or a named agent for or on behalf of the master.

Any signature by the carrier, master or agent must be identified as that of the carrier, master or agent.

Any signature by an agent must indicate whether the agent has signed for or on behalf of the carrier or for or on behalf of the master.

ii. indicate that the goods have been dispatched, taken in charge or shipped on board at the place stated in the credit, by:

—pre-printed wording, or

—a stamp or notation indicating the date on which the goods have been dispatched, taken in charge or shipped on board.

The date of issuance of the transport document will be deemed to be the date of dispatch, taking in charge or shipped on board, and the date of shipment. However, if the transport document indicates, by stamp or notation, a date of dispatch, taking in charge or shipped on board, this date will be deemed to be the date of shipment.

iii. indicate the place of dispatch, taking in charge or shipment and the place of final destination stated in the credit, even if:

— the transport document states, in addition, a different place of dispatch, taking in charge or shipment or place of final destination, or

—the transport document contains the indication "intended" or similar qualification in relation to the vessel, port of loading or port of discharge.

iv. be the sole original transport document or, if issued in more than one original, be the full set as indicated on the transport document.

v. contain terms and conditions of carriage or make reference to another source containing the terms and conditions of carriage (short form or blank back transport document). Contents of terms and conditions of carriage will not be examined.

vi. contain no indication that it is subject to a charter party.

b. For the purpose of this article, transshipment means unloading from one means of conveyance and reloading to another means of conveyance (whether or not in different modes of transport) during the carriage from the place of dispatch, taking in charge or shipment to the place of final destination stated in the credit.

c.（略）

i. A transport document may indicate that the goods will or may be transshipped provided that the entire carriage is covered by one and the same transport document.

ii. A transport document indicating that transshipment will or may take place is acceptable, even if the credit prohibits transshipment.

UCP 600 第 19 条　涵盖至少两种不同运输方式的运输单据

a.涵盖至少两种不同运输方式的运输单据（多式或联合运输单据），无论名称如何，必须在表面上看来：

i. 表明承运人名称并由以下人员签署：

— 承运人或其具名代理人，或

— 船长或其具名代理人。

承运人、船长或代理人的任何签字，必须标明其承运人、船长或代理人的身份。

代理人签字必须标明其系代表承运人还是船长签字。

ii. 通过以下方式表明货物已经在信用证规定的地点发送、接管或已装运。

— 事先印就的文字；或者

— 表明货物已经被发送、接管或装运日期的印戳或批注。

运输单据的出具日期将被视为发送、接管或装运的日期，也即发运的日期。然而如单据以印戳或批注的方式表明了发送、接管或装运日期，该日期将被视为发运日期。

iii. 表明信用证规定的发送、接管或发运地点，以及最终目的地，即使：

— 该运输单据另外还载明了一个不同的发送、接管或发运地点或最终目的地；或者

— 该运输单据载有"预期的"或类似的关于船只、装货港或卸货港的限

定语。

iv. 为唯一的正本运输单据,或者,如果出具为多份正本,则为运输单据中表明的全套单据。

v. 载有承运条款和条件,或提示承运条款和条件参见别处(简式/背面空白的运输单据)。银行将不审核承运条款和条件的内容。

vi. 未表明受租船合同约束。

b. 就本条而言,转运指在从信用证规定的发送、接管或者发运地点至最终目的地的运输过程中从某一运输工具上卸下货物并装上另一运输工具的行为(无论其是否为不同的运输方式)。

c.(略)

i. 运输单据可以表明货物将要或可能被转运,只要全程运输由同一运输单据涵盖。

ii. 即使信用证禁止转运,注明将要或者可能发生转运的运输单据仍可接受。

UCP 600 – Article 20:Bill of Lading

a. A bill of lading, however named, must appear to:

i. indicate the name of the carrier and be signed by:

— the carrier or a named agent for or on behalf of the carrier, or

— the master or a named agent for or on behalf of the master.

Any signature by the carrier, master or agent must be identified as that of the carrier, master or agent.

Any signature by an agent must indicate whether the agent has signed for or on behalf of the carrier or for or on behalf of the master.

ii. indicate that the goods have been shipped on board a named vessel at the port of loading stated in the credit by:

— pre-printed wording, or

— an on board notation indicating the date on which the goods have been shipped on board.

The date of issuance of the bill of lading will be deemed to be the date of shipment unless the bill of lading contains an on board notation indicating the date of shipment, in which case the date stated in the on board notation will be deemed to be the date of shipment.

If the bill of lading contains the indication "intended vessel" or similar qualification in relation to the name of the vessel, an on board notation indicating the date of shipment and the name of the actual vessel is required.

iii. indicate shipment from the port of loading to the port of discharge stated in the credit.

If the bill of lading does not indicate the port of loading stated in the credit as the port of loading, or if it contains the indication "intended" or similar qualification in relation to the port of loading, an on board notation indicating the port of loading as stated in the credit, the date of shipment and the name of the vessel is required. This provision applies even when loading on board or shipment on a named vessel is indicated by pre-printed wording on the bill of lading.

iv. be the sole original bill of lading or, if issued in more than one original, be the full set as indicated on the bill of lading.

v. contain terms and conditions of carriage or make reference to another source containing the terms and conditions of carriage (short form or blank back bill of lading). Contents of terms and conditions of carriage will not be examined.

vi. contain no indication that it is subject to a charter party.

b. For the purpose of this article, transshipment means unloading from one vessel and reloading to another vessel during the carriage from the port of loading to the port of discharge stated in the credit.

c. (略)

i. A bill of lading may indicate that the goods will or may be transshipped provided that the entire carriage is covered by one and the same bill of lading.

ii. A bill of lading indicating that transshipment will or may take place is acceptable, even if the credit prohibits transshipment, if the goods have been shipped in a container, trailer or LASH barge as evidenced by the bill of lading.

d. Clauses in a bill of lading stating that the carrier reserves the right to transship will be disregarded.

UCP600 第 20 条　提单

a. 提单,无论名称如何,必须看似:

i. 表明承运人名称,并由下列人员签署:

— 承运人或其具名代理人,或者

— 船长或其具名代理人。

Chapter 6　Ocean Transport

承运人、船长或代理人的任何签字必须标明其承运人、船长或代理人的身份。

代理人的任何签字必须标明其系代表承运人还是船长签字。

ii. 通过以下方式表明货物已在信用证规定的装货港装上具名船只：

—预先印就的文字，或

—已装船批注注明货物的装运日期。

提单的出具日期将被视为发运日期，除非提单载有表明发运日期的已装船批注，此时已装船批注中显示的日期将被视为发运日期。

如果提单载有"预期船只"或类似的关于船名的限定语，则需以已装船批注明确发运日期以及实际船名。

iii. 表明货物从信用证规定的装货港发运至卸货港。

如果提单没有表明信用证规定的装货港为装货港，或者其载有"预期的"或类似的关于装货港的限定语，则需以已装船批注表明信用证规定的装货港、发运日期以及实际船名。即使提单以事先印就的文字表明了货物已装载或装运于具名船只，本规定仍适用。

iv. 为唯一的正本提单，或如果以多份正本出具，为提单中表明的全套正本。

v. 载有承运条款和条件，或提示承运条款和条件参见别处（简式/背面空白的提单）。银行将不审核承运条款和条件的内容。

vi. 未表明受租船合同约束。

b. 就本条而言，转运系指在信用证规定的装货港到卸货港之间的运输过程中，将货物从一船卸下并再装上另一船的行为。

c.（略）

i. 提单可以表明货物将要或可能被转运，只要全程运输由同一提单涵盖。

ii. 即使信用证禁止转运，注明将要或可能发生转运的提单仍可接受，只要其表明货物由集装箱、拖车或子船运输。

d. 提单中声明承运人保留转运权利的条款将被不予理会。

UCP 600 – Article 31　Partial Drawings or Shipments

a. Partial drawings or shipments are allowed.

a. 答应分批支款或分批装运。

b. A presentation consisting of more than one set of transport documents evidencing shipment commencing on the same means of conveyance and for the same journey, provided they indicate the same destination, will not be regarded as covering a partial shipment, even if they indicate different dates of shipment or different ports of loading, places of taking in charge or dispatch. If the presentation consists of more than one set of transport documents, the latest date of shipment as evidenced on any of the sets of transport documents will be regarded as the date of shipment.

b. 表明使用同一运输工具并经由同次航程运输的数套运输单据在同一次提交时,只要显示相同目的地,将不视为部分发运,即使运输单据上标明的发运日期不同或装卸港、接管地或发送地点不同。假如交单由数套运输单据构成,其中最晚的一个发运日将被视为发运日。

A presentation consisting of one or more sets of transport documents evidencing shipment on more than one means of conveyance within the same mode of transport will be regarded as covering a partial shipment, even if the means of conveyance leave on the sance day for the same destination.

含有一套或数套运输单据的交单,假如表明在同一种运输方式下经由数件运输工具运输,即使运输工具在同一天出发运往同一目的地,仍将被视为部分发运。

c. A presentation consisting of more than one courier receipt, post receipt or certificate of posting will not be regarded as a partial shipment if the courier receipts, post receipts or certificates of posting appear to have been stamped or signed by the same courier or postal service at the same place and date and for the same destination.

c. 含有一份以上快递收据、邮政收据或投邮证实的交单,假如单据看似由同一快递或邮政机构在同一地点和日期加盖印戳或签字并且表明同一目的地,将不被视为部分发运。

Exercise

Ⅰ. Blank-filling
1. 提单按照收货人抬头不同分为(　　)、(　　)、(　　)。
2. 按签发提单时货物是否装船来分,提单分为(　　)和(　　)。
3. 在我国出口贸易中,通常采用凭指定空白背书提单,习惯上称之为"(　　)"。

Chapter 6　Ocean Transport

Ⅱ. *Multiple choice*

1. 解释"W/M plus ad val"的含义(　　)。
   A. 货物重量或尺码　　B. 货物重量加尺码　　C. 货物重量、尺码或价值选较高的
   D. 货物重量或尺码选较高的再加上从价运费
2. 国际贸易中,海运提单的签发日期是指(　　)。
   A. 货物开始装船的日期　　　　　　　B. 货物全部装船完毕的日期
   C. 货物装船完毕船舶启航日期
3. 必须经过背书才能进行转让的提单是(　　)。
   A. 记名提单　　　　　B. 不记名提单　　　　　C. 指示提单
4. 海运提单和航运提单两种运输单据(　　)。
   A. 都是物权凭证　　　B. 都是可转让的物权凭证
   C. 前者是物权凭证可以转让,后者不是物权凭证不可以转让
5. 出口人完成装运后,凭以向船公司换取已装船提单的单据是(　　)。
   A. Shipping Order　　　B. Mate's Receipt　　　C. Freight Receipt
6. 国际贸易中最主要的运输方式是(　　)。
   A. 航空运输　　　B. 铁路运输　　　C. 海洋运输　　　D. 公路运输
7. 班轮运送货物,如果运费计收标准为"A.V",则表示(　　)。
   A. 按货物毛重计收　　　　　　　　B. 按货物体积计收
   C. 按商品价格计收　　　　　　　　D. 按货物件数计收
8. 某出口商品每件净重 30kg,毛重 34kg,体积每件 40cm×30cm×20cm。如果班轮运价计费标准为 W/M10 级,则船公司计收运费时应按(　　)。
   A. 毛重计收　　　　　　　　　　　B. 净重计收
   C. 体积计收　　　　　　　　　　　D. 价值计收
9. 在进出口业务中,能够作为物权凭证的运输单据有(　　)。
   A. 铁路运单　　　B. 海运提单　　　C. 航空运单　　　D. 邮包收据
10. 在业务中,出口商完成装运后,凭(　　)向船公司换取正式提单。
    A. 发货单　　　B. 收货单　　　C. 大副收据　　　D. 商业发票
11. 装运期的规定办法通常有(　　)。
    A. 明确规定具体装运期限　　　　B. 规定在收到信用证后若干天
    C. 规定在某一天装运完毕　　　　D. 笼统规定近期装运
12. 在国际贸易中,开展以集装箱运输的国际多式联运,有利于(　　)。
    A. 简化发运手续　　　　　　　　B. 加快货运速度
    C. 降低运输成本　　　　　　　　D. 提高货运质量

13. 按运输方式分,提单有( )。
    A. 直运提单　　　　B. 转船提单　　　　C. 联运提单　　　　D. 舱面提单
14. 按照提单收货人抬头的不同,提单可分为( )。
    A. 已装船提单　　　B. 指示提单　　　　C. 记名提单　　　　D. 不记名提单

Ⅲ. True or false statements

1. 不清洁提单是说提单上有污渍。
2. 海运提单的签发日期是指货物开始装船的日期。
3. 海运提单、铁路提单、航空运单都是物权凭证,都是可以通过背书转让。
4. 某商品每箱体积为 30cm×40cm×50cm,毛重为 62kg,如果班轮运费计收的标准为 W/M,则船公司应该按照尺码吨计算运费有利。
5. 铁路运单、航空运单性质上与海运提单相同,都可作为物权凭证在市场上流通转让。
6. 我出口公司按照合同的规定于 8 月 1 日发运了货物并取得提单,于 8 月 30 日向银行提交全套合格单据要求付款。按照 UCP600 的规定,只要未超过信用证有效期,银行就有义务付款。
7. 清洁提单是指不载有任何批注的提单。
8. 业务中常用的"空白抬头"的提单是指在提单收货人栏中不填写任何内容。

Ⅳ. Answering short questions

1. 买卖合同中的装运条款包括哪些内容?装运时间如何规定?
2. 什么叫提单?提单的性质和作用如何?
3. 何谓"空白抬头、空白背书"提单?何谓清洁提单和不清洁提单?对结汇有何影响?

Ⅴ. Calculation

1. 我公司出口到某国家商品 1000 箱,每箱体积 40cm×30cm×20cm,毛重为 30kg。经查,该商品计费标准为 W/M,等级为 10 级,每吨运费率为 200 港币。另查得到该国要加收港口附加费 20%。问:我方应付轮船公司运费多少?
2. 我公司出口商品 200 件,每件毛重 95kg,体积 100cm×40cm×25cm,查轮船公司运费表,该商品计费标准为 W/M,等级为 8 级,每吨运费为 80 美元,另收港口附加费 10%,直航附加费 15%。问:该批货物共计运费多少?我方原报 FOB 上海每件 400 美元,客户要求改报 CFR 价,我方应报多少?

Chapter 6　Ocean Transport

Ⅵ. *Case study*

1. 我某进出口公司对外出口 100 箱货物，货物按时装运并取得清洁提单，货到目的港卸货时，发现只有 90 箱，卖方为此扣 10 箱货款，是否有道理？

2. 上海运往肯尼亚蒙巴萨港口"门锁"一批计 100 箱，每箱体积为 20cm×30cm×40cm，毛重为 25kg。燃油附加费为 30%，蒙巴萨港口拥挤附加费为 10%。门锁属于小五金类，计算标准是 W/M，等级为 10 级，基本运费为每吨运费 443 港元，试计算运费为多少？

3. 英国进口方 A 租用船方 B 的船运送一批进口的中国柑橘，双方约定该船应直接驶往利物浦。但 B 方签发的提单上写明："船可以用任何方式，经由任何航线驶往目的港"。实际上该船先到了比利时的一个港口后，再到利物浦时正赶上英国提高进口柑橘的关税，而且大批中国柑橘已到货，市场价格下跌，A 方因此受到损失，于是向法院起诉 B 违约。

4. A Chinese exporter exported 5000 sets electrical household appliances to an importer on the basis of USD 600 per set CFR Los Angeles. Both parties agreed to stipulate the following in the contract:

　　"....40% payment by T/T in advance and 60% payment by time L/C.

　　The buyer should remit the 40% of total value on or before September 30th, 2008.

　　Shipment from Chinese port to Los Angeles not later than Oct. 21th, 2008.

　　Packed in wooden box fumigated more over 12 hours.

　　Partial shipment and transshipment are prohibited...."

After receiving buyer's remittance money on September 28th, the exporter shipped 3000 sets in Shanghai Port on Oct. 4th, 2008, then sent shipping advice on time to the importer and got one set of clean on board B/Ls. Then the exporter shipped the other 2000 sets on board the same vessel in Guangzhou Port on Oct. 8th, 2008, sent shipping advice on time to the importer and got other one set of clean on board B/Ls. And then the vessel began to sail to Los Angeles.

Whether the seller has breached the contract provision of "Partial shipment and transshipment are prohibited" or not? Why?

Chapter 7 Insurance

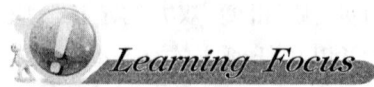

Risks, losses and expenses
Coverages under ICC
W/W clause (commencement and termination of the insurance)
Insurance clause in contract
Insurance policy

7.1 Risks, Losses and Expenses

According to the loss or damage caused by risks included in different coverages and the expenses involved, the insurance company is responsible for indemnifying the insured goods. Obviously, risk, loss and expense are closely related to each other. In order to have a clear understanding of the contents of insurance, these three terms should be clarified.

7.1.1 Risks

Risks are divided into two types to be covered by ocean marine cargo insurance. The first type is the perils of the sea, which include both natural calamities and fortuitous accidents. It should be noted that all the perils must occur at sea and must be because of sea; Otherwise, they are not covered by the insurance. For example:

   natural calamities 自然灾害   heavy weather 恶劣天气
   lightning 雷电   tsunami 海啸
   earthquake 地震   volcanic eruption 火山爆发
   fortuitous accidents 意外事故   ship stranded 船舶搁浅

striking upon the rocks 触礁   ship sinking 船沉
ship collision 船舶互撞   fire 火灾
explosion 爆炸   ship missing 船只失踪

The second type of risks is extraneous risks which include ordinary risks such as theft, pilferage, rain damage, shortage, breakage, etc. and special risks such as strike, war, failure to delver, etc.

7.1.2 Losses

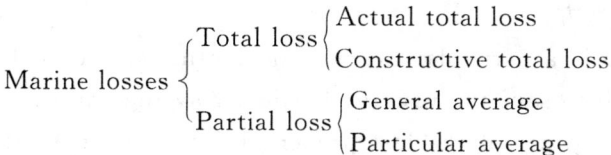

Ocean marine cargo insurance covers two types of losses: total loss（全部损失）and partial loss（部分损失）.

Total loss can be divided into actual total loss and constructive total loss. Actual total loss means the non-existence of the insured cargo in value. Constructive total loss, however, means the subject matter insured is reasonably abandoned due to its actual total loss appearing to be unavoidable or because it would not be preserved from actual total loss without an expenditure greater than its recovered value. In other words, it is unlikely to recover the subject matter or the cost of recovery will exceed the value of the subject matter.

Case study：

e.g. (1) 我公司出口稻谷一批,因保险事故被海水浸泡多时而丧失其原有价值,货到目的港后只能低价出售,这种损失属于<u>实际全损</u>。

e.g. (2) 有一批出口服装,在海上运输途中,因船体触礁导致服装严重受浸,若将这批服装漂洗后运至原定目的港所花费的费用已超过服装的保险价值,这种损失属于<u>推定全损</u>。

e.g. (3) 有一台精密仪器价值 15 000 美元,货轮在航行途中触礁,船身剧烈震动而使仪器受损。事后经专家检验,修复费用为 16 000 美元,如拆为零件销售,可卖 2000 美元。问该仪器属于何种损失？

【分析提示】

该种损失属于推定全损。因为其修理、恢复费用和续运费用总和大于货物本身的价值。

Partial loss means the total loss of part of the insured cargo or the damage to all or part of the insured cargo. It is classified into general average(共同海损)and particular average(单独海损).

General average is a loss that affects all cargo interests on the ship and the ship itself. It means that whichever shipper loses all or part of his cargo, all the other will club together to recompense him for his loss. It is the minimum coverage in general use.

共同海损的分摊(General Average Contribution):共同海损分摊时,涉及的受益方包括货方、船方和运费方。

However, when there is a particular average loss, other interests do not need to sacrifice their cargo to save the voyage. Particular average means a loss that is borne solely by the owner of the lost property(ship or cargo). Partial damage of cargo by sea water is, for instance, a particular average, while partial damage of cargo by water that has been used to put out a fire is a general average because the damage has been made in order to save both the ship and the cargo on board the ship of all the cargo owners.

Case study:

e.g. (1) 一艘船在途经某海峡时起火,造成部分商品烧毁,船长在命令救火过程中又造成部分商品湿毁。烧毁的商品损失是什么损失?湿毁的商品损失是什么损失?

e.g. (2) 某货轮从天津新港驶往新加坡,航行途中船舶货舱起火,大火蔓延到机舱,船长为了船货的共同安全,决定采取紧急措施,往舱中灌水灭火。火虽被扑灭,但由于主机受损无法继续航行,于是船长决定雇用拖轮拖回新港修理,检修后重新驶往新加坡。事后调查,这次事故造成的损失为:

(a) 1000 箱货物被火烧毁。

(b) 600 箱货物由于灌水灭火而受损。

(c) 主机和部分甲板被烧坏。

(d) 拖轮费用和额外增加的燃料及船长、船员的工资。

试分析以上损失分别属于什么性质的损失?

共同海损和单独海损的区别:造成海损的原因不同;承担损失的责任不同。

Chapter 7 Insurance

7.1.3 Expenses

Ocean marine insurance also covers some expenses incurred in reducing the loss of the subject matter insured either by the assured himself or a party other than the insured. This is intended to encourage efforts to save the subject matter insured.

7.2 Coverages under CIC

China Insurance Clauses were made effective on January 1, 1981 and are now offered by PICC Property and Casualty Company Limited. They are the most commonly used insurance clauses in China.

7.2.1 Basic insurance coverages

7.2.1.1 Free from particular average (FPA)

Free from particular average literally means no partial loss or damage is recoverable. According to PICC's Ocean Marine Cargo Clause, it really covers:

(1) Total loss of cargo together with ship or aircraft by natural calamities;

(2) Total or partial loss caused by accidents;

(3) Partial loss of the insured goods attributable to heavy weather, lightening, where the conveyance has been grounded, stranded, sunk or burnt;

(4) Partial or total loss consequent on falling of entire package or packages into sea during loading, transshipment or discharge;

(5) Reasonable cost incurred by the insured in salvaging the goods or averting or minimizing a loss recoverable under the Policy, provided that such cost shall not exceed the sum insured of the consignment so saved;

(6) Losses attributable to discharge of the insured goods at a port of distress following a sea peril as well as special charges arising from loading, warehousing and forwarding of the goods at an intermediate port of call or refuge;

(7) Sacrifice in and contribution to general average and salvage charges;

(8) Such proportion of losses sustained by the shipowners as is to be reimbursed by the cargo owner under the Contract of Affreightment "Both to Blame Collision" clause.

7.2.1.2 With particular average(WPA)

WPA covers wider than FPA. Aside from the risks covered under FPA conditions as above, this insurance also covers partial loss of the insured goods caused by heavy weather, lightening, tsunami, earthquake and/or flood. The relationship between FPA and WPA can be described as follows:

$$W.P.A = F.P.A + \text{partial loss due to natural calamities}$$

7.2.1.3 All Risks(AR)

The cover of All Risks is the most comprehensive of the three. Aside from the risks covered under FPA and WPA conditions as above, this insurance also covers all risks of loss of or damage to the insured goods whether partial or total, arsing from external causes in the course of transit. It should be noted that "All Risks" does not, at its name suggests, really cover all risks. The "All Risks" clause excludes coverage against damage caused by war, strikes, riots, etc. The relationship between WPA and All Risks can be described as follows:

$$AR = W.A + \text{losses due to general external causes}$$

7.2.2 Additional insurance coverage

If more protections are needed, the cargo owner may further insure the goods against one or several additional risks. However, no additional risk can be purchased to insure goods independently. Additional risks include general additional risks and special additional risks. Since the scope of cover of general additional risks is already included into that of All Risks, it is not necessary for the goods to be insured by general additional risks if it is insured by All Risks.

7.2.2.1 General additional risks

(1) Theft, pilferage and non-delivery clause

(2) Fresh water and/or rain damage clause

(3) Shortage clause

(4) Intermixture and contamination clause

(5) Leakage clause

(6) Clash and breakage clause

(7) Taint of odor clause

(8) Sweat and heating clause

(9) Hook damage clause

(10) Breakage of packing clause

(11) Rust clause

7.2.2.2　Special additional risks

(1) War risk

(2) Strike risk

(3) On deck risk

(4) Import duty risk clause

(5) Rejection risk

(6) Aflatoxin risk

(7) Failure to deliver clause

(8) Fire risk extension clause for storage of cargo at destination Hong Kong, including Kowloon or Macao

7.3　W/W Clause (commencement and termination of the insurance)

"仓至仓条款"(warehouse to warehouse,简称 W/W),即保险公司所承担的保险责任,是从被保险货物运离保险单所载明的起运港(地)发货人仓库开始,一直到货物到达保险单所载明的目的港(地)收货人的仓库时为止。当货物一进入收货人仓库,保险责任即行终止。但是,当货物从目的港卸离海轮时起算满60天,不论保险货物有没有进入收货人的仓库,保险责任均告终止。

Insurance will be effective as soon as the insured goods are taken away from the warehouse listed on the IP. The insurance will terminate when the goods are carried to the final warehouse listed on the IP, or it exceeds 60 days after the goods are unloaded from the ship in case they fail to reach the warehouse during a reasonable period of time.

在FOB和CFR条件下,保险责任起讫实际上是"船"至"仓"。因为虽由买方投保,但依照风险划分界限,买方一般不会办理货物装船前的保险。只有在CIF价格术语下,保险责任起讫才是真正的"仓"至"仓"。因为,此时保险由卖方办理,自货物运离起运地仓库到越过船舷为止,货损是由卖方承担的(拥有可保利益)。

Case study:

(1)卖方A与买方B订立了一份FOB合同,货物在装船后,卖方向买方发出装船合同,买方已向保险公司投保"一切险",采用"仓至仓条款"。但货物在从卖方仓库运往码头的途中,因意外事故而致10%货物受损,事后卖方以保险单含有"仓至仓条款",要求保险公司赔偿,但遭保险公司拒绝。后来卖方又请求买方以买方的名义凭保险单向保险公司提赔,但同样遭保险公司拒绝。

(2)上海某单位以CIF条件从国外进口某货物一批,卖方已代办了一切险。该批货物在上海卸货后,当晚在码头被偷窃。买方能否向保险公司要求赔偿?

【分析提示】

可以向保险公司索赔。因为一切险中包含有偷窃提货不着险,而且一切险采用的"仓至仓条款",当晚在码头被偷窃产生的损失,应该在保险公司赔偿责任范围之内。

7.4 Insurance Clause in Contract

(1)保险由买方负责。

Insurance to be effected by the Buyer.

(2)投保一切险和战争险按CIF价发票金额的110%计算。

Insurance to be covering All Risks and War Risk for 110% of CIF invoice value.

(3)卖方负责按发票金额110%投保平安险,买方如果要附加其他险,由买方自行投保并承担费用。

Insurance to be effected by the Seller against F. P. A for 110% of the CIF invoice value, any additional insurance required by the Buyer shall be effected by him at his own expense.

(4)按发票金额的110%投保水渍险和偷盗、提货不着险,战争险。如果发生索赔,则在纽约以美元支付。

战争险的保险费按0.1%计算,如果成交后,保险费用超过0.1%,那么超额部分由买方负责,如果无人承保战争险,卖方可不保此险。因此,信用证上必须作出以下规定:

"如果战争险的保险费超过0.1%,受益人有权收取超过信用证金额部分的保险费,或不投保此险。"

Insurance to cover WPA plus TPND and war risks for 110% of the CIF value and to provide for claims, if any, payable in New York in US currency.

War risks premium is calculated at 0.1%, if it is higher than 0.1% after the conclusion of contract, the excess premium shall be for Buyer's account and if war risks insurance is not obtainable, Seller may be exempted from providing such insurance. Therefore, L/C must include following clause:

"If war risks premium is higher than 0.1%, beneficiary is authorized to draw the difference in excess of L/C amount, or to exempt from providing such insurance."

(5)"保险由卖方按发票金额的×××%投保×××险、×××险,以中国人民保险公司有关海洋运输货物保险条款为准。

Insurance to be effected by the seller for 110% of invoice value against All Risks as per Marine Cargo Clause of the PICC of China.

7.5 Insurance Policy

7.5.1 Major types of insurance policy

Insurance policy, issued by the insurer, is a legal document setting out the exact terms and conditions of an insurance transaction—the name of the insured, the name of commodity insured, the amount insured, the name of the carrying vessel, the precise risks covered, the period of cover and any exceptions there. It also serves as a written contract of insurance between the insurer and the person taking out insurance. An insurance policy forms part of the chief shipping documents.

The major types of marine insurance policies are:

Time Policy A time policy is taken for definite period of time, usually not exceeding 12 months say from January 1, 2015 to December 31, 2015. This policy is most suitable for hull insurance.

Voyage Policy Where the subject matter is insured for a specific voyage, say from Karachi to Port Saeed it is named as voyage policy.

Mixed Policy This policy is the combination of time and voyage policy. It, therefore, covers the risks for both particular voyage and for a stated period of time.

Floating Policy Floating policy is taken for a relatively large sum by the regular suppliers of goods. It covers several shipments which are declared afterwards along with other particulars. This policy is most situated to exporter in order to avoid trouble of taking out a separate policy for every shipment.

Valued Policy Under its terms, the agreed value of the subject matter of insurance is mentioned in the policy itself. In case of cargo, this value means the cost of goods plus freight and shipping charges plus 10% to 15% margin for anticipated profit. The said value may be more than the actual value of goods.

Un-valued Policy（Open Policy） Where the value of the subject matter of insurance is not declared but left to be ascertained and proved later it is called unvalued policy.

7.5.2 Sample of insurance policy

中国人民保险公司
THE PEOPLE'S INSURANCE COMPANY OF CHINA
总部设于北京　　1949年创立
Head Office：Beijing Established in 1949
保险单
INSURANCE POLICY

发票号码　　　　　　　　　　　　保险单号次
Invoice No. _____　　　　　Policy No. _____

　　中国人民保险公司（以下简称本公司），根据_____（以下简称被保险人）的要求，由被保险人向本公司缴付约定的保险费，按照本保险单承保险别和背面所载条款与下列特别条款承保下述货物运输，特立本保险单。

　　This Policy of Insurance witnesses that the People's Insurance Company of China (hereinafter called "the Company"), at the request of _____ (hereinafter called "the Insured") and in consideration of the agreed premium being paid to the company by the Insured, undertake to insure the undermentioned goods in transportation subject to the conditions of this policy as per the clause printed overleaf and other special clauses attached hereon.

标记 Marks & Nos.	包装及数量 Quantity	保险货物项目 Description of Goods	保险金额 Amount Insured

总保险金额
Total amount insured _____

保费　　　　　　　　费率　　　　　　　　装载工具
Premium as arranged　Rate as arranged　Per conveyance S. S _____

开航日期　　　　　　　自　　　　　　　　至
Slg. On or abt: _____　from _____　to _____

承保险别
Conditions

所保货物，如遇危险，本公司凭本保险单及其他有关证件给付赔款。

Claims, if any, payable on surrender of this Policy together with other relevant documents.

所保货物，如发生本保险单项下负责赔偿的损失或事故，应立即通知本公司下述代理人查勘。

In the event of accident whereby loss or damage may result in a claim under this Policy immediate notice applying for survey must be given to the company's agent as mentioned hereunder:

中国人民保险公司
THE PEOPLE'S INSURANCE COMPANY OF CHINA

赔偿偿付地点
Claim payable at _____

日期
Date _____

知识链接

UCP 600 – Article 28　Insurance Document and Coverage

a. An insurance document, such as an insurance policy, an insurance certificate or a declaration under an open cover, must appear to be issued and signed by an insurance company, an underwriter or their agents or their proxies.

Any signature by an agent or proxy must indicate whether the agent or proxy has signed for or on behalf of the insurance company or underwriter.

b. When the insurance document indicates that it has been issued in more than one original, all originals must be presented.

c. Cover notes will not be accepted.

d. An insurance policy is acceptable in lieu of an insurance certificate or a declaration under an open cover.

e. The date of the insurance document must be no later than the date of shipment, unless it appears from the insurance document that the cover is effective from a date not later than the date of shipment.

f. (略)

i. The insurance document must indicate the amount of insurance coverage and be in the same currency as the credit.

ii. A requirement in the credit for insurance coverage to be for a percentage of the value of the goods, of the invoice value or similar is deemed to the minimum amount of coverage required.

If there is no indication in the credit of the insurance coverage required, the amount of insurance coverage must be at least 110% of the CIF or CIP value of the goods.

When the CIF or CIP value can not be determined from the documents, the amount of insurance coverage must be calculated on the basis of the amount for which honour or negotiation is requested or the gross value of the goods as shown on the invoice, whichever is greater.

iii. The insurance document must indicate that risks are covered at least between the place of taking in charge or shipment and the place of discharge or final destination as stated in the credit.

g. A credit should state the type of insurance required and, if any, the additional risks to be covered. An insurance document will be accepted without regard to any risks that are not covered if the credit uses imprecise terms such as "usual risks" or "customary risks".

h. When a credit requires insurance against "all risks" and an insurance document is presented containing any "all risks" notation or clause, whether or not bearing the heading "all risks", the insurance document will be accepted without regard to any risks stated to be excluded.

i. An insurance document may contain reference to any exclusion clause.

j. An insurance document may indicate that the cover is subject to a franchise or excess(deductible).

Chapter 7 Insurance

UCP600 第 28 条   保险单据及保险范围

a. 保险单据,例如保险单或预约保险项下的保险证明书或者声明书,必须由保险公司或承保人或其代理人或代表出具并签署。

代理人或代表的签字必须标明其系代表保险公司或承保人签字。

b. 如果保险单据表明其以多份正本出具,所有正本均须提交。

c. 暂保单将不被接受。

d. 可以接受保险单代替预约保险项下的保险证明书或声明书。

e. 保险单据日期不得晚于发运日期,除非保险单据表明保险责任不迟于发运日生效。

f.（略）

i. 保险单据必须表明投保金额并以与信用证相同的货币表示。

ii. 信用证对于投保金额为货物价值、发票金额或类似金额的某一比例的要求,将被视为对最低保额的要求。

如果信用证对投保金额未作规定,投保金额须至少为货物的 CIF 或 CIP 价格的 110%。

如果从单据中不能确定 CIF 或者 CIP 价格,投保金额必须基于要求承付或议付的金额,或者基于发票上显示的货物总值来计算,两者之中取金额较高者。

iii. 保险单据须标明承包的风险区间至少涵盖从信用证规定的货物监管地或发运地开始到卸货地或最终目的地为止。

g. 信用证应规定所需投保的险别及附加险(如有的话)。如果信用证使用诸如"通常风险"或"惯常风险"等含义不确切的用语,则无论是否有漏保之风险,保险单据将照样被接受。

h. 当信用证规定投保"一切险"时,如保险单据载有任何"一切险"批注或条款,无论是否有"一切险"标题,均将被接受,即使其声明任何风险除外。

i. 保险单据可以援引任何除外责任条款。

j. 保险单据可以注明受免赔率或免赔额(减除额)约束。

Exercise

Ⅰ. Blank filling

1. 海上风险一般包括(　　　)和(　　　)。
2. 海上损失根据损失的程度分为(　　　)和(　　　)。
3. CIC 是(　　　)的英文简称,根据中国人民保险公司规定基本险包括(　　　)、(　　　)、(　　　)。

4. 附加险别主要包括（　　　）、（　　　）。
5. 按照损失的性质，可将海损分为（　　　）和（　　　）两种。
6. 海上运输货物保险保障的费用主要有（　　　）和（　　　）两种。
7. 根据我国《海洋运输货物保险条款》，海运货物保险险别分为（　　　）和（　　　）两类。
8. 根据我国现行的《海洋货物运输保险条款》的规定，在基本险别中包括（　　　）、（　　　）和（　　　）三种。
9. 根据中国人民保险公司海洋运输货物保险条款规定，保险公司对基本险承保的责任起讫均采用的是（　　　）。
10. 保险公司对战争险保险期限仅限于（　　　）或运输工具危险。
11. 根据我国《海洋运输货物保险条款》，海运货物的索赔期限，从被保险货物运抵目的港全部卸离海轮之日起算，最多不超过（　　　）。

Ⅱ. *Multiple choice*

1. 以下属于一般附加险的是（　　　）。
　　A. 战争险　　　B. 钩损险　　　C. 淡水雨淋险　　　D. 短量险　　　E. 罢工险
　　F. 进口关税险　　G. 黄曲霉素险　　　　H. 串味险
2. 在海运货物保险业务中，共同海损是属于（　　　）。
　　A. 全部损失的一种　　B. 部分损失的一种　　C. 单独海损的一种
3. 某外贸公司以 CIF 条件与国外客户达成一笔出口业务，由出口商负责投保，按照《2010 年通则》应投保（　　　）。
　　A. 一切险　　　　　B. 水渍险　　　　　C. 平安险
4. 仓至仓条款（　　　）。
　　A. 出口人负责交货责任起讫的条款　　　B. 承运人负责交货责任起讫的条款
　　C. 保险人负责交货责任起讫的条款
5. 按照中国保险条款的规定，一切险的责任范围是指（　　　）加上一般外来原因所致的全部和部分损失。
　　A. 水渍险的责任范围　　B. 平安险的责任范围　　C. 平安险和水渍险的责任范围
6. 某公司按 CIF 条件出口坯布 1000 包，货物在途中因货舱淡水管道漏水遭到 150 包货物水渍，保险公司对下列那种险别负责投保（　　　）。
　　A. 一切险　　　　　B. 水渍险　　　　　C. 平安险
7. 按照中国人民保险公司海运货物保险条款的做法，投保一切险后，还可以投保（　　　）。
　　A. 偷窃提货不着险　　B. 卖方利益险　　C. 战争、罢工险
8. 为了防止运输途中货物被偷窃，应该投保（　　　）。

A. 偷窃提货不着险　　　　B. 一切险　　　　　C. 一切险加保偷窃险

D 水渍险加保偷窃险　　　E 平安险加保偷窃险

9. 土畜产公司出口肠衣一批,为了防止在运输途中因为容器破坏引起渗漏损失,保险应该投保(　　)。

A. 渗漏险　　　　　　　B. 一切险　　　　　C. 一切险加保渗漏险

D. 水渍险加保渗漏险　　E. 平安险加保渗漏险

10. 国外来证规定:"最迟装运期为 2009 年 9 月 15 日,有效期 2009 年 9 月 30 日,单据必须在提单日后 15 天提交",若提单的出单日期为 2009 年 9 月 10 日,则保险单据的出单日期应为(　　)。

A. 2009 年 9 月 10 日　　　　　　　B. 2009 年 9 月 10 日以前

C. 2009 年 9 月 15 日以前　　　　　D. 2009 年 9 月 25 日以前

E. 2009 年 9 月 30 日以前

11. 在保险人所承保的海上风险中,雨淋、渗漏属于(　　)。

A. 自然灾害　　　B. 意外事故　　　C. 一般外来风险　　　D. 特殊外来风险

12. 在海运过程中,被保险物被海盗劫持造成的损失属于(　　)。

A. 实际全损　　　B. 推定全损　　　C. 共同海损　　　D. 单独海损

13. 船舶搁浅时,为使船舶脱险而雇佣驳船强行脱浅所支出的费用,属于(　　)。

A. 实际全损　　　B. 推定全损　　　C. 共同海损　　　D. 单独海损

14. 某海贸公司出口茶叶 5 公吨,在海运途中遭受暴风雨,海水涌入舱内,致使一部分茶叶发霉变质,这种损失属于(　　)。

A. 实际全损　　　B. 推定全损　　　C. 共同海损　　　D. 单独海损

15. 战争、罢工风险属于(　　)。

A. 自然灾害　　　B. 意外事故　　　C. 一般外来灾害　　　D. 特殊外来风险

16. 我公司按 CIF 条件出口棉花 300 包,货物在海运途中因货舱内水管渗漏,致使 50 包棉花遭水渍受损,在投保下列哪种险别时,保险公司负责赔偿(　　)。

A. 平安险　　　B. 水渍险　　　C. 战争险　　　D. 一切险

17. 根据我国《海洋货物运输保险条款》的规定,承保范围最小的基本险别是(　　)。

A. 平安险　　　B. 水渍险　　　C. 一切险　　　D. 罢工险

18. 我公司按 FOB 进口一批玻璃器皿,在运输途中的装卸、搬运过程中,部分货物受损。要得到保险公司赔偿,我公司应该投保(　　)。

A. 平安险　　　B. 一切险　　　C. 破碎险　　　D. 一切险加破碎险

19. 根据现行伦敦保险协会《海运货物保险条款》的规定,采用"一切风险减除外责任"的办法表示的险别是(　　)。

A. ICC(A)　　　B. ICC(B)　　　C. ICC(C)　　　D. ICC(D)

20. 根据现行伦敦保险协会《海运货物保险条款》的规定,承保风险最大的险别是( )。
   A. ICC(A)　　　　B. ICC(B)　　　　C. ICC(C)　　　　D. ICC(D)

21. 根据现行伦敦保险协会《海运货物保险条款》规定,下列险别中,不能单独投保的是( )。
   A. ICC(A)　　　　B. 战争险　　　　C. ICC(C)　　　　D. 恶意损害险

22. 根据"仓至仓条款"的规定,从货物在目的港卸离海轮时起满多少天,不管货物是否进入保险单载明的收货人仓库,保险公司的保险责任均告终止( )。
   A. 15 天　　　　B. 30 天　　　　C. 10 天　　　　D. 60 天

23. 在海上保险业务中,构成被保险货物"实际全损"的情况有( )。
   A. 保险标的物完全灭失　　　　B. 保险标的物丧失已无法挽回
   C. 保险标的物发生变质,失去原有使用价值
   D. 船舶失踪达到一定时期

24. 我公司以 CFR 条件进口一批货物,在海运途中部分货物丢失。要得到保险公司赔偿,我公司可投保( )。
   A. 平安险　　　　　　　　　　B. 一切险
   C. 平安险加保偷窃提货不着险　　D. 一切险加保偷窃提货不着险

25. 根据我国现行《海洋货物运输保险条款》的规定,能够独立投保的险别有( )。
   A. 平安险　　　　B. 水渍险　　　　C. 一切险　　　　D. 战争险

26. 根据我国现行《海洋货物运输保险条款》规定,下列损失中,属于水渍险承保范围的有( )。
   A. 由海啸造成的被保货物的损失
   B. 由于下雨造成的被保货物的损失
   C. 由于船舱淡水水管渗漏造成的被保货物的损失
   D. 由于船舶搁浅造成的被保货物的损失

Ⅲ. True of false statements

1. 全部损失分为共同海损和单独海损。( )
2. 一切险承保的是所有海上风险。( )
3. 水渍险承保的是淡水水渍引起的损失。( )
4. 在平安险中不包括自然灾害引起的部分损失。( )
5. 陆运运输保险主要险别包括陆运险、陆运一切险两种。( )
6. 在航空运输险中,已经加保了战争险,再加保罢工险,不另收保险费。( )
7. 按照我国《海洋货物运输保险条款》的规定,三种基本险和战争险均使用"仓至仓

条款"。（   ）
8. 在国际贸易中，向保险公司投保一切险后，在运输途中由于任何外来原因造成的一切货损，均可向保险公司索赔。（   ）
9. "仓至仓条款"就是船公司负责将货物从装运地发货人的仓库运送到目的地收货人的仓库的运输条款。（   ）
10. 偷窃、提货不着险和交货不到险均在一切险的范围内，只要投保一切险，收货人如果提不到货，保险公司均应该负责赔偿。（   ）
11. 托运出口玻璃制品时，被投保人在投保一切险后，还应该投保破碎险。（   ）
12. 出口茶叶在装运途中，最大的问题就是怕串味，因此，保险时应该投保串味险。（   ）
13. 某外贸公司按 CIF 术语出口坯布 1000 包，根据合同规定投保水渍险，货在途中因为船舱内淡水管道滴漏，致使该批坯布中的 200 包遭水渍，保险公司应对此负责赔偿。（   ）
14. 海上保险业务中的意外事故，仅局限于发生在海上的意外事故。（   ）
15. 船舶失踪达到半年以上可作推定全损处理。（   ）
16. 单独海损是由承保风险所直接造成的被保险货物的部分损失。（   ）
17. 共同海损是部分海损中的一种。（   ）
18. 共同海损要由受益各方根据获救利益大小按比例分摊。（   ）
19. 当被保险货物遭受承保范围内的灾害事故时，由保险人或被保险人以外的第三者采取救助行为而花费的费用叫施救费用。（   ）
20. 因为共同海损属于部分海损，所以在投保平安险的情况下，对于由于自然灾害产生的共同海损，保险公司是不负责赔偿的。（   ）
21. "一切险"的承保范围包括由自然灾害、意外事故以及一切外来风险所造成的被保险货物的损失。（   ）

Ⅳ. Answering short questions

1. 在海运货物保险中，保险公司分别承保哪几类风险、损失与费用？
2. 什么叫共同海损？什么叫单独海损？两者有何区别？
3. 我某公司以 CIF 对外发盘，如以下列保险条款投保，是否妥当？
    - 一切险、淡水雨淋险、受潮受热险。
    - 平安险、一切险、战争险。
    - 水渍险、偷窃险、战争险。
    - 偷窃险、罢工险、战争险。
4. 出口合同中的保险条款应包括哪些内容？

5. 某批货物投保了水渍险,载运该批货物的海轮在航行中遇到下雨,而使货物遭到水渍损失。试问在上述情况下,保险公司是否负责赔偿?为什么?
6. 我出口公司对非洲某客商发盘,供应某商品,价格条件为 CIF 非洲某口岸每公吨 500 美元,按发票金额 110% 投保一切险和战争险。对方要求改报 FOB 中国口岸,经查自中国口岸至非洲某口岸的海洋运费为每公吨 150 美元,一切险费率为 2.3%,战争险费率为 5‰。问 FOB 价应报多少?

Ⅴ. Calculation

1. 某公司出口货一批,单价为 1200 美元/公吨 CIF 纽约,按发票金额的 110% 投保,投保一切险,保险费率为 0.8%。现在客户要求改报 CFR 价格,计算在不影响我国收汇的前提下,应该报价多少?
2. 报价某商品 CIF 旧金山 2000 美元/公吨,按发票金额的 110% 投保,费率合计 0.6%,客户要求按发票金额的 130% 投保,我们应该如何报价?

Ⅵ. Case study

1. 海轮的舱面上装有 1000 台拖拉机,航行中遇大风浪袭击,450 台拖拉机被卷入海中,海轮严重倾斜,如不立即采取措施,则有翻船的危险,船长下令将余下的 550 台拖拉机全部抛入海中。请问:这 1000 台拖拉机的损失属于何种性质?
2. 有一台精密仪器价值 15 000 美元,货轮在航行途中触礁,船身剧烈震动而使仪器受损。事后经专家检验,修复费用为 16 000 美元,如拆为零件销售,可卖 2000 美元。问该仪器属于何种损失?
3. 有批货物已投保了平安险,该货在装船过程中有 8 件落海,其中 5 件因打捞及时,仅造成部分损失,其余 3 件全部灭失。在这种情况下,保险公司应赔偿几件货物?
4. 一批货物已投保了平安险,分装两艘货轮驶往目的港。一艘货轮在航行中遇暴风雨袭击,船身颠簸,货物相互碰撞而发生部分损失;另一艘货轮在航行中则与流冰碰撞,货物也发生了部分损失。请问:保险公司对于这两次的损失是否都应给予赔偿?
5. 上海某单位以 CIF 条件从国外进口某货物一批,卖方已代办了一切险。该批货物在上海卸货后,当晚在码头被偷窃。买方能否向保险公司要求赔偿?
6. 一批货物已经按发票总值的 110% 投保了平安险。货轮在航行途中于 5 月 3 日遇暴风雨袭击,该批货物受到部分水滞,损失货值 1000 元人民币;该轮在继续航行中又于 5 月 8 日触礁,货物再次发生部分损失,损失额亦为 1000 元人民币。在这种情况下,保险公司应赔偿多少钱?为什么?

7. 我国某进出口公司向挪威出口一批货物,装于某某号货轮上。同一货轮上还有日本和韩国的货物,三家货物的价值分别为:60万元、75万元和80万元。船在航行途中触礁,船身底部发现一处裂口,涌入大量海水,致使舱内部分货物遭水浸泡。船长命令将船驶向浅滩进行修补,而后为了起浮又将部分笨重货物抛入海中,请问:在这些损失中,哪些属于共同海损,哪些又是单独海损?

8. 某货物在运输过程中起火,大火蔓延到机舱,船长下令往舱内灌水灭火,火虽被扑灭,但由于主机受损,无法继续航行,于是,船长决定雇用拖轮将货船拖到附近港口修理。事后调查。造成的损失有:(1)1000 箱货被火烧毁;(2)600 箱货由于灌水灭火受到损失;(3)主机和部分甲板被烧毁;(4)额外增加的燃油和船长、船员的工资。试分析以上各种损失的性质,并指出至少应投保何种险别,保险公司才负责赔偿?

9. 有一货轮在航行中与流冰相撞,船身一侧裂口,船内部分乙方商品遭浸泡,船长不得不将船就近驶入浅滩,进行排水修补裂口,而后为了浮起船只,又将部分笨重货物抛入海中,船体撞裂和部分乙方货物遭受浸泡损失了3万美元,将船舶驶向浅滩以及产生的一连串损失共为8万美元。试问:应如何分摊这些损失?(已知:获救后的船舶价值为100万美元;船上货物甲、乙、丙三家货物价值分别为50万美元、30万美元、8万美元;待收运费2万美元)

10. 某外贸公司按 CIF 术语出口一批货物,装运前已向保险公司按发票总值的110%投保平安险,6月初货物装妥顺利开航。载货船舶于6月13日在海上遇到暴风雨,致使一部分货物受到水渍,损失价值为2100美元。数日后,该轮又突然触礁,致使该批货物又遭到部分损失,损失价值为8000美元。问:保险公司对该批货物的损失是否赔偿?为什么?

11. 某货物从天津新港驶往新加坡,在航行途中船舶货舱起火,大火蔓延到机舱,船长为了船、货的共同安全,决定采取紧急措施,往舱内灌水灭火。火虽然被扑灭,但由于主机受损,无法继续航行,于是船长决定雇佣拖轮将货船拖回新港修理。检修后重新驶往新加坡。事后调查,这次事件造成的损失有:(1)1000箱货被火烧毁;(2)600箱货由于灌水灭火受到损失;(3)主机和部分甲板烧毁;(4)拖船费用;(5)额外增加的燃料和船长、船员的工资。从上述各项损失性质来看,各属于什么海损?

12. 某公司以 CFR 上海从国外进口一批货物,并据卖方提供的装船通知及时向中国人民保险公司投保水渍险,后来由于国内用户发生变更,我进口公司通知承运人货改卸黄浦港。在货由黄浦装火车运往南京途中遇到山洪,致使部分货物受损,我进口公司据此向保险公司索赔但遭拒绝。保险公司拒赔有无道理?说明理由。

Chapter 8 Payment

Means of payment
Modes of payment

8.1 Lead in Practice

8.1.1 Words and phrases about price in foreign trade

unit price	attractive price
best price	cheap price
competitive price	favorable price
home market price	import/export price
international market price	keen price
lowest price	moderate price
prevailing price	reasonable price
retail price	rock-bottom price
wholesale price	

1. 随函附上我方报价单。
Enclosed is your price list.
2. 价格肯定上涨。
Prices are bound to go up.
3. 若你方愿意降低价格,比方说 5%,我们愿向你方试定此货。
Should you be prepared to reduce the price by, say, 5%, we should place trial order with you.

4. 鉴于我们已按此价与买方大量成交，我们不可能再降价了。

In view of the fact that we have done a lot of business with buyers at this price, we can not reduce our price any further.

5. 我们建议你方再次重新考虑发价，使之与国际市场价格一致。

We suggest that you reconsider your price, and bring it into line with the international market price.

6. 我方决定再作2%的让步，希望这能有助于你方推销产品。

We have decided to make a further concession of 2% in the hope that this will help you push the sales of our products.

7. 很遗憾即使再让一半，我们仍难以接受你方还盘。

We regret that it is impossible to accept your counteroffer, even to meet you halfway.

8. 有迹象表明市场进一步看涨。

Information shows that the market will advance further.

9. 你方报价过高。

The price you offered is rather stiff.

10. 我方不知你方价格是否有所变动。

I wonder whether there are any changes in your price.

8.1.2 Compose a dialogue on the following situation

Commodity: silk

Price: USD 100 per long ton

Quantity: 50 long tons

Payment: by irrevocable L/C at sight

The buyer asks for a 8% reduction in the price. The seller refuses to consider any reduction, but gives a 2% commission. Finally they conclude the business.

8.2 Means of Payment

8.2.1 Bill of exchange

8.2.1.1 Definition of B/E

B/E, also called draft, is an unconditional order in writing, addressed by one person(drawer) to another(drawee), signed by the person giving it, requiring the person to whom it is addressed to make payment on demand, or at a fixed or determinable future time, a sum certain in money, to, or to the order of a specified person(payee), or to "bearer".

汇票是由一人开致另一人的书面的无条件命令,由发出命令的人签名,要求接受命令的人立即,或在固定的时间,或在可以确定的将来时间,把一定金额的货币支付给一个特定的人,或他的指定人,或来人。

A draft should involve three parties: namely, drawer, drawee and payee.

8.2.1.2 Components of B/E

The following samples of draft can help to make clear the content of it.

No. 7088

$ 10,000　　　　　　New York, 8th January, 2012

　On demand pay to Tom Smith or bearer the sum of USD Ten Thousand only.

To: Mr. Green
　　London

　　　　　　　　　　　　　　　　　　　　　　(signed) David White

No. 677/96

Exchange for $ 7,500　　　　Shanghai, China, 8th August, 2012

　At for 60 days sight of this exchange pay to or to the order of Shanghai Import and Export Corporation the sum of USD Seven Thousand only.

To: ABC Import and Export Co., Ltd.
　　　　　　　　　　　Shanghai Import and Export Corporation
　Miami, USA
　　　　　　　　　　　　　　　　Manager
　　　　　　　　　　　　　　　　(signed)

The two samples may be decomposed into the following elements:

(1) Draft number

Make out according to the invoice number or fill in "AS PER INVOICE".

Chapter 8　Payment

(2) Place and date

Fill in the drawer's address and issuing date.

(3) Amount

Fill in currency and figures.

e. g. USD7,200.00, Stg 3,600.00, DM7,500.00, JPY 4,620.00,etc.

(4) Tenor

There are two kinds of tenor: payment at sight and payment in future time. If it is the former, "At Sight" is to be printed. If it is the latter, to print "At ×××　days after sight","At ××× days after date of draft" or "At ××× days after date of B/L or on stipulated date".

(5) Payee

Usually three kinds of writings:

Restrictive Order　　Make out "pay ××× company only". This kind of bill can not be negotiable.

Demonstrative Order　　Make out "pay ××× company's order" or "pay to the order of ××× company". This kind of bill can be negotiable with endorsement.

Payable to Bearer　　It is negotiable without endorsement.

(6) Amount

Fill in capital words and currency.

It should be in accordance with (3), otherwise the bank will refuses to pay. For example:

SAY U.S. Dollars SEVEN THOUSAND TWO HUNDRED ONLY,

SAY POUND STERLING THREE THOUSAND SIX HUNDREND ONLY.

(7) Payer or drawee

It is usually the issuing bank under a letter of credit.

(8) Drawer

The drawer is the principal on collection terms, while it is the beneficiary on L/C terms. The drawer should keep in accordance with the stipulation of L/C completely. The draft is null and void without signature and seal of the drawer.

8.2.1.3　Classification of B/E

(1) Commercial bill and banker's bill

A bill of exchange can be classified into commercial bill and banker's bill according to different drawers. If the drawer is a commercial firm, the bill is called a commercial bill. It is often used in foreign trade finance. If the drawer is a bank, the bill is called a banker's bill. It is mainly used in remittance.

(2) Sight bill and time bill

According to the time when the bill falls due, bills of exchange may be divided into sight bill (demand bill) and time bill (usance bill). A sight draft requires the drawee to pay the bill on demand or at sight. A time bill requires the drawee to accept it at first and pay it at a fixed or determinable future time.

(3) Clean bill and documentary bill

Clean bill is a draft to which no documents are attached. It is usually used to collect commission, interests, sample fee and cash in advance. However, if a draft is presented with some shipping documents attached, such as bill of lading, insurance policy, invoice, etc., the draft is called documentary bill which is used to collect payment of import and export goods.

8.2.1.4　Use of B/E

A draft starts from issue. The operation process of draft includes: to draw, presentation, acceptance, payment, endorsement, dishonor and recourse. The procedure of B/E depends on the two types of draft, which is shown as follows:

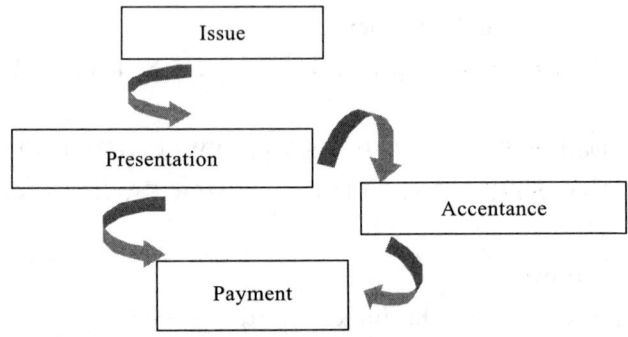

Here are the explanations of these terms:

Presentation: The holder of a draft shows and hands it over to the drawee for acceptance or payment.

Acceptance: A draft is said to be accepted when the drawee signs name on it, by putting the word "accepted", plus the date of acceptance, thus undertaking to pay the value of the draft to the payee at a specified future date.

Endorsement: The placing of one's signature on the reverse of a commercial document primarily for the purpose of transferring the rights of the document holder to some other person.

Question: If a holder presents a time draft which is not due, can he get immediate payment? If he wants to get immediate payment in this case, how can he do?

Discount: A percentage deduction made for cash payment, e. g. Against a draft before its maturity.

Dishonor: A draft is said to be dishonored when the drawee refuses or is unable to pay the amount due, or accept the draft.

Discourse: If a draft is dishonored, the holder of the draft can exercise his right of recourse and ask the drawer or the endorser to pay the draft amount.

Assignment
按照下列提供的信用证摘要和有关数据编制送银行议付的汇票一份。
(1) Summary of L/C.
    CREDITO ITALIANO BANK, Milan, Italy
    Irrevocable Credit No. 500/21212—44, Date: May 22, 2011.
    Beneficiary: China National Textiles I/E corp. Beijing.
We hereby issue in your favor this irrevocable documentary credit which is available by your draft drawn on us at 90 days after date of B/L for full invoice value accompanied by the following documents:
Draft should bear our credit number and date.
Draft must be negotiated not later than June 30, 2011.
(2) Invoice No. 91/A128 dated June 14, 2011.
Invoice value: USD 140, 814. 18.
(3) Goods shipped on June 18, 2011.
(4) Negotiating bank: Bank of China, Beijing Branch.

8.2.2 Promissory note

A promissory note is an unconditional promise in writing made by one person to another signed by the maker, engaging to pay, on demand or at a fixed or determinable future, a sum certain in money, to or to the order of a specified person or to bearer.

The main difference between a promissory note and a draft lies in that there are three parties, namely drawer, drawee and payee involved in a draft but only two, drawer and payee in a promissory note. The payer of promissory note is the drawer himself.

8.2.3 Check

A check is an unconditional order in writing drawn on a bank signed by the drawer, requiring the bank to pay on demand a sum certain in money to or to the order of a specified person or to bearer.

A check is a special kind of draft which is drawn on a bank and paid on demand.

8.3 Modes of Payment

8.3.1 Remittance

Under remittance, the payer instructs his bank or other institutions to have a payment made to the payee. There are four parties involved in the remittance business: the remitter, the payee, the remitting bank and the paying bank. Remittance is usually used in the sales under the terms of cash in advance, cash with order, cash on delivery or open account.

8.3.1.1 M/T

For mail transfer, the buyer (the remitter) gives money to his bank (remitting bank) which then, issues a trust deed for payment and sends it to the correspondent bank (paying bank) in the seller's place by mail instructing him to pay the amount to the seller. This method costs less, but much slower.

8.3.1.2 T/T

The process of telegraphic transfer is similar to M/T except that the instructions from the buyer's bank to the paying bank are made by SWIFT[①] instead of

---

[①] SWIFT: (Society for Worldwide Interbank Financial Telecommunication)环球同业银行金融电信协会.

by mail. This means that payment can be made more efficiently. Furthermore, SWIFT makes T/T a cheap and popular method of payment nowadays.

8.3.1.3 D/D

Under demand draft, the remitting bank, at the request of the buyer, draws a sight draft on the paying bank instructing it to make payment to the seller on behalf of the buyer. It is a cheaper but slower method of transferring funds from a local bank.

8.3.2 Collection

Under collection, the exporter entrusts the remitting bank(托收行) to collect the price from the buyer through its collecting bank(代收行). In the course of collection, banks only provide the service of collecting and remitting, and are not liable for non-payment of the importer.

8.3.2.1 D/P at sight

(1) The exporter sends the draft together with shipping documents to the remitting bank.

(2) The remitting bank sends the draft and shipping documents to a correspondent bank overseas—the collecting bank.

(3) The collecting bank presents the sight bill and documents to the importer for payment.

(4) The importer makes payment.

(5) The collecting bank hands over the documents to the importer.

(6) The collecting bank notifies the remitting bank of crediting the money to their account.

(7) The remitting bank makes payment to the exporter.

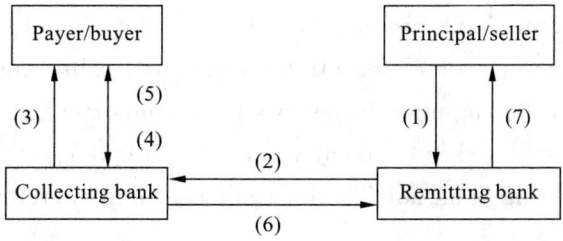

8.3.2.2 D/P after sight

(1) The exporter sends the draft together with shipping documents to the remitting bank.

(2) The remitting bank sends the draft and shipping documents to a correspondent bank overseas—the collecting bank.

(3) The collecting bank presents the bill and documents to the importer for acceptance. After the importer accepts the draft, the collecting bank takes back the draft and documents.

(4) The importer makes payment when time falls due.

(5) The collecting bank hands over the documents to the importer.

(6) The collecting bank notifies the remitting bank of crediting the money to their account.

(7) The remitting bank makes payment to the exporter.

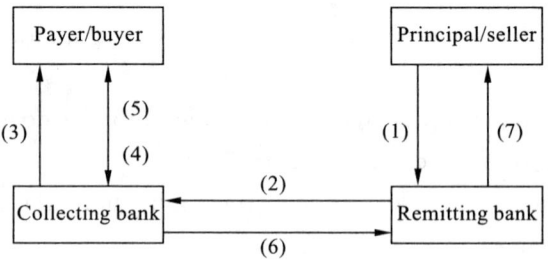

8.3.2.3 D/A

(1) The exporter sends the draft together with shipping documents to the remitting bank.

(2) The remitting bank sends the draft and shipping documents to a correspondent bank overseas—the collecting bank.

(3) The collecting bank presents the draft and documents to the importer for acceptance. After the importer accepts the draft, the collecting bank takes back the draft and gives the shipping documents to the importer.

(4) The importer makes payment when time falls due.

(5) The collecting bank notifies the remitting bank of crediting the money to their account.

(6) The remitting bank makes payment to the exporter.

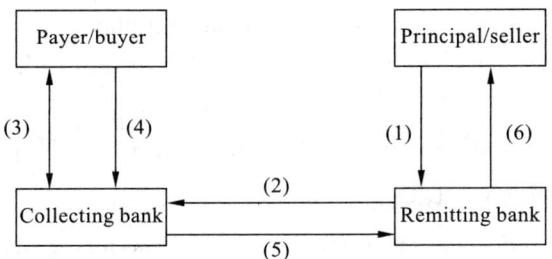

8.3.2.4 D/P·T/R

For D/P after sight and D/A, there are disadvantages to Both Parties:

To seller: He can not get immediate payment.

To buyer: He can not get documents immediately.

In this case, trust receipt can be used under D/P, and the method of payment is called D/P·T/R.

Trust Receipt 进口方借单时提供的一种书面信用担保文件,用来表示愿意以代收行的受托人身份代为提货、报关、保险、出售等并承认货物所有权仍属于银行,出售后的货款应于汇票到期日时交银行,这是代收行向进口方提供的信用便利,与出口人无关。

It allows the buyer to take possession of goods, the collecting bank retains the title to the goods.

Case study:

出口方委托银行以远期付款交单方式向进口方代收货款。货到目的地后,进口方凭信托收据向代收行借取了全套货运单据先行提货销售,但因经营不善而亏损,无法向银行支付货款。至此,出口方应向何方追偿?为什么?

Remittance and collection belong to the commercial credit. "Credit" stipulates who takes responsibility of paying money and surrendering the shipping documents that represent the title to the goods. In remittance and collection transaction, the buyer is responsible for making payment, the seller handing over the documents. Therefore, the seller would suffer a risk and the payment is not guaranteed by the bank.

8.3.3 Letter of credit

Case study:

"The beneficiary's drafts drawing at 120 days after sight are to be paid in face amount as drawn at sight basis as discounting charges, acceptance commissions and usance interests are for account of the accountee". Which L/C bears such remarks?

If a L/C does not state it is transferable, is it a transferable credit?

8.3.3.1　Definition of L/C

The letter of credit is a letter addressed to the seller, written and signed by a bank acting on behalf of the buyer. The bank promises that it will pay or accept drafts drawn on itself if the seller conforms exactly to the conditions set forth in the letter of credit. Only the documents submitted are in conformity with the letter will the bank pay or accept the exporter's draft.

信用证是开证行根据申请人的要求，向受益人开立的有一定金额的在一定期限内凭规定单据在指定的地点支付的书面保证。信用证实质上是银行代表其客户（买方）向卖方有条件地承担付款责任的凭证。

Question：What are the parties involved in L/C?

(1)开证申请人(Applicant/buyer)

Liable for payment to the issuing bank provided no discrepancy between documents and the credit;

Right to examine the documents and refuse payment;

Any requirement of the applicant should be satisfied by certain documents and clearly indicated when making credit application.

(2)开证行(Issuing bank/the buyer's bank)

By issuing a credit, the issuing bank undertakes full responsibility for payment.

(3)受益人(Beneficiary/seller)

The right to examine a credit upon receipt of it according to the sales contract;

Whether be paid or not solely depends on the fulfillment of terms and conditions of the credit.

(4)通知行(Advising bank/transmitting bank)

Accurately transmit the terms of credit and check the apparent authenticity of the credit.

(5)保兑行(Confirming bank)

Undertake the same obligations assumed by the issuing bank;

Responsible for a credit independently and pay without recourse.

(6)议付行(Negotiating bank)

In a negotiation credit, purchases the drafts and documents;

When dishonored by the issuing bank, it has the right of recourse to the beneficiary;

Obtain the reimbursement from the issuing bank.

(7)付款行(Paying/accepting bank)

Designated by issuing bank to effect payment or acceptance, in most cases to be the advising bank;

Once it has made payment to the beneficiary, it will lose the right of recourse to the beneficiary;

Entitled to obtain reimbursement from the issuing bank.

(8)偿付行(Reimbursing bank)

A bank named in credit from which the paying bank, accepting bank or negotiating bank may request cover after paying or negotiating the documents.

The reimbursing bank shall not examine the documents.

8.3.3.2 Contents of L/C

Sample of Letter of Credit

Issue of a Documentary Credit

BKCHCNBJA08E SESSION:000 ISN:000000
BANK OF CHINA
LIAONING
NO. 5 ZHONGSHAN SQUARE
ZHONGSHAN DISTRICT
DALIAN
CHINA——开证行

Destination Bank:
KOEXKRSESXXX MESSAGE TYPE:700
KOREA EXCHANGE BANK
SEOUL
178.2KA, ULCHI RO, CHUNG-KO——通知行

Type of Documentary Credit	40A	IRREVOCABLE——信用证性质为不可撤销
Letter of Credit Number	20	LC84E0081/99——信用证号码,一般做单时都要求注此号
Date of Issue	31G	990916——开证日期
Date and Place of Expiry	31D	991015 KOREA——失效时间、地点
Applicant Bank	51D	BANK OF CHINA LIAONING BRANCH——开证行
Applicant	50	DALIAN WEIDA TRADING CO., LTD.——开证申请人
Beneficiary	59	SANGYONG CORPORATION CPO BOX 110 SEOUL KOREA——受益人
Currency Code, Amount	32B	USD 1,146,725.04——信用证总额
Available with...by...	41D	ANY BANK BY NEGOTIATION——任何银行议付 有的信用证为 ANY BANK BY PAYMENT
Drafts at	42C	45 DAYS AFTER SIGHT——见证45天内付款
Drawee	42D	BANK OF CHINA LIAONING BRANCH——付款行
Partial Shipments	43P	NOT ALLOWED——分装不允许
Transshipment	43T	NOT ALLOWED——转船不允许
Shipping on Board/Dispatch/Packing in Charge at/ from	44A	RUSSIAN SEA——起运港
Transportation to	44B	DALIAN PORT, P. R. CHINA——目的港
Latest Date of Shipment	44C	990913——最迟装运期
Description of Goods or Services:	45A	——货物描述

FROZEN YELLOWFIN SOLE WHOLE ROUND（WITH WHITE BELLY）USD 770/MT CFR DALIAN QUANTITY：200MT

ALASKA PLAICE（WITH YELLOW BELLY）USD 600/MT CFR DALIAN QUANTITY：300MT

Documents Required：46A——议付单据

1. SIGNED COMMERCIAL INVOICE IN 5 COPIES.

   ——签字的商业发票5份。

2. FULL SET OF CLEAN ON BOARD OCEAN BILLS OF LADING MADE OUT TO ORDER AND BLANK ENDORSED, MARKED "FREIGHT PREPAID" NOTIFYING LIAONING OCEAN FISHING CO., LTD. TEL：(86)411-3680288.

   ——一整套清洁已装船提单,抬头为 TO ORDER 的空白背书,且注明运费已付,通知人为 LIAONING OCEAN FISHING CO., LTD. TEL：(86)411-3680288。

3. PACKING LIST/WEIGHT MEMO IN 4 COPIES INDICATING QUANTITY/GROSS AND NET WEIGHTS OF EACH PACKAGE AND PACKING CONDITIONSAS CALLED FOR BY THE L/C.

   ——装箱单/重量单4份,显示每个包装产品的数量/毛、净重和信用证要求的包装情况。

4. CERTIFICATE OF QUALITY IN 3 COPIES ISSUED BY PUBLIC RECOGNIZED SURVEYOR.

   ——由 PUBLIC RECOGNIZED SURVEYOR 签发的质量证明3份。

5. BENEFICIARY'S CERTIFIED COPY OF FAX DISPATCHED TO THE ACCOUNTEE WITH 3 DAYS AFTER SHIPMENT ADVISING NAME OF VESSEL, DATE, QUANTITY, WEIGHT, VALUE OF SHIPMENT, L/C NUMBER AND CONTRACT NUMBER.

   ——受益人证明的传真件,在船开后3天内已将船名航次、日期、货物的数量、重量、价值、信用证号和合同号通知付款人。

6. CERTIFICATE OF ORIGIN IN 3 COPIES ISSUED BY AUTHORIZED INSTITUTION.

   ——当局签发的原产地证明3份。

7. CERTIFICATE OF HEALTH IN 3 COPIES ISSUED BY AUTHORIZED INSTITUTION.

   ——当局签发的健康/检疫证明3份。

ADDITIONAL INSTRUCTIONS: 47A——附加指示。

1. CHARTER PARTY B/L AND THIRD PARTY DOCUMENTS ARE ACCEPTABLE.

——租船提单和第三方单据可以接受。

2. SHIPMENT PRIOR TO L/C ISSUING DATE IS ACCEPTABLE.

——装船期早于信用证的签发日期是可以接受的。

3. BOTH QUANTITY AND AMOUNT 10 PERCENT MORE OR LESS ARE ALLOWED.

——允许数量和金额公差在10%左右。

Charges	71B	ALL BANKING CHARGES OUTSIDE THE OPENNING BANK ARE FOR BENEFICIARY'S ACCOUNT.
Period for Presentation	48	DOCUMENTSMUST BE PRESENTED WITHIN 15 DAYS AFTER THE DATE OF ISSUANCE OF THE TRANSPORT DOCUMENTS BUT WITHIN THE VALIDITY OF THE CREDIT.
Confirmation Instructions	49	WITHOUT

Instructions to the Paying/Accepting/Negotiating Bank: 78

1. ALL DOCUMENTS TO BE FORWARDED IN ONE COVER, UNLESS OTHERWISE STATED ABOVE.

2. DISCREPANT DOCUMENT FEE OF USD 50.00 OR EQUAL CURRENCY WILL BE DEDUCTED FROM DRAWING IF DOCUMENTS WITH DISCREPANCIES ARE ACCEPTED.

"Advising Through" Bank	57A	KOE×KRSE××× MESSAGE TYPE: 700 KOREA EXCHANGE BANK, SEOUL, 178.2 KA, ULCHI RO, CHUNG-KO.

• About the L/C itself

(1) Form of L/C

(2) L/C number

(3) Date of issue and expiry

Chapter 8 Payment

(4) L/C amount

(5) Parties in L/C

• About the goods

(1) Commodity name, article number and specification

(2) Quantity, packing and unit price

• About the shipping documents

(1) Documents required

(2) If necessary, time of tendering shipping documents（如果不规定交单期，出口方必须在提单日期后 21 天之内交单）

Case study：

我国某公司与外商签订一份以信用证方式支付的 CIF 出口合同。对方来证规定：装运期不得迟于 8 月 5 日，信用证有效期为 8 月 31 日。我公司 8 月 28 日向议付行提交签发日期 8 月 5 日的提单，却遭到议付行拒付。请问议付行拒付有没有道理？

• About the transportation

(1) Time of shipment

(2) Transshipment and partial shipment

(3) Port of loading and port of discharge

• About B/E

(1) Drawer

(2) Drawee

(3) Tenor

8.3.3.3 Circulation of L/C

The following shows the procedure of sight negotiation L/C：

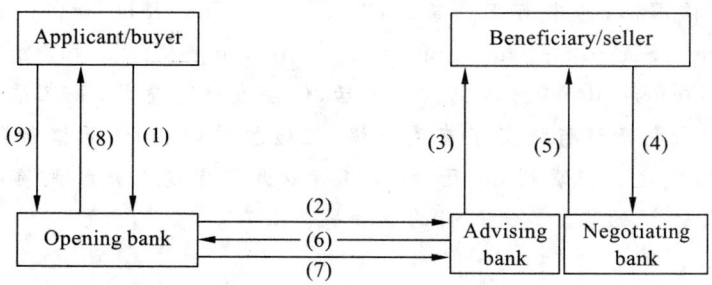

(1) The buyer makes application for a letter of credit with his bank and signs the opening bank's agreement form. The opening bank approves the application and issues the actual letter of credit document.

(2) The opening bank forwards the letter of credit to the advising bank.

(3) The advising bank delivers the letter of credit to the beneficiary.

(4) Having examined the letter of credit, the beneficiary ships the goods to the buyer. After that, the beneficiary prepares documents, draws a draft and presents them to his bank.

(5) The beneficiary's bank negotiates the documents and pays funds to the beneficiary in accordance with the letter of credit.

(6) The negotiating bank forwards the documents to the opening bank.

(7) The opening bank receives the documents and checks them. If the documents are in order and comply with the letter of credit, the opening bank credits the negotiating bank's account.

(8) The opening bank notifies the buyer to make payment for documents.

(9) After making payment, the buyer receives the documents and takes delivery of the goods.

8.3.3.4　Features of L/C

Case study:

(1) 中东某商人从西欧购买一项商品，买卖双方约定采用信用证付款方式，并明确分两批交货和分两批开立信用证。第一张信用证开出后，已顺利结汇。第二张信用证开出后，买方因第一批货物质量有问题，向卖方索赔的事尚未了结，便通知银行停止使用其已开出的第二张不可撤销的信用证，但银行仍凭卖方第二批交货的正确单据付了款。当银行通知买方对第二批交货付款赎单时，遭到买方拒绝，银行遂向法院起诉，你认为法院将如何判决？

(2) 中国某外贸公司按信用证付款方式出售一批货物，买方通过日本银行开来不可撤销的信用证，其中有下列条款："credit amount USD 50 000 according to invoice value: 75% to be paid at sight, the remaining 25% to be paid at 60 days after shipment arrival."卖方收到信用证后，依法发运了货物，并在信用证有效期内，通过议付行向开证行提交了有关单据，经检验单证相符，开证行即付75%货款，计 37 000 美元。但货到 60 天后，开证行以开证申请人声称到货品质欠佳为由，拒付其余 25% 的货款。开证行的做法是否正确？

From the case above, what features do you think L/C boasts?

Chapter 8　Payment

- The issuing bank has the first responsibility to make payment.
- L/C is an unattached document, that is, it is not attached to the sales contract.
- The business of L/C is not based on goods but on documents.

8.3.3.5　Examination and Amendment of L/C

Question: what is the purpose of examination of L/C?

Case study:

Write a letter of amending L/C.

正昌公司业务员仔细核对,查出以下不符之处。

审证结果:

(1)信用证大小写金额不一致,大写金额错误,应为 US Dollars twenty four thousand eight hundred and twenty only 而不是 US Dollars twenty four thousand eighteen hundred and twenty only。

(2)投保加成率为 20%,高于售货确认书规定的 10%。

(3)投保险别为一切险,与售货确认书规定的一切险加战争险不同。

(4)售货确认书中不允许分批装运,但信用证中允许分批装运。

(5)装运期最迟是 2001 年 2 月 28 日,而不是 3 月 11 日。

根据上述审证意见,拟写改证函。

Zhengchang Trading Co., Ltd.

FM: 86-572-2371522

TO: 0094-01-827653

DT: 6th Jan, 2001

Dear Mr. Stock,

Thank you for your L/C No. copsilo0000103 issued by Bank of Ceylon Colombo.

After going through the L/C, we have found the following discrepancies with our Sales Confirmation No. ZCTC1212/00:

(1) The amount in words is different form that in figure. The former is wrong according to the Sales Confirmation. The correct is US Dollars Twenty Four Thousand Eight Hundred and Twenty only.

(2) The goods are insured for 110% of invoice value, not 120%.
(3) Insurance Certificate Covering all risks and War Risk not against all risks.
(4) According to the Sales Confirmation, the partial shipment is not allowed.
(5) The Latest Date of Shipment is 28-FEB-2001, not 11-MARCH-2001.

Please let us have your L/C Amendment soon so that we can effect shipment within the latest delivery time.
Best wishes!

Yours truly,
Zhengchang Trading Co., Ltd.
Li Hua

8.3.3.6 Classifications of L/C

(1) Confirmed L/C and unconfirmed L/C

A confirmed credit has the commitment of the confirming bank besides that of issuing bank. The payment is guaranteed by both issuing bank and confirming bank. Therefore, the exporter has double assurance of payment and is better protected. An advising bank will not confirm a credit unless it is required to do so. A confirming credit is used when the issuing bank's credit standing is unknown or questionable.

An unconfirmed credit has the commitment of the issuing bank only. There is no undertaking on the part of advising bank or any other bank.

(2) Sight L/C, usance L/C, usance L/C payable at sight

(a) Sight L/C

—Sight payment documentary credit

A sight payment documentary credit will nominate the paying bank which is to pay, without recourse, the stipulated sum immediately against presentation to it of the required documents. A draft is not essential for this credit.

—Sight negotiation documentary credit

Chapter 8　Payment

According to UCP 600, negotiation means the purchase by the nominated bank of drafts (drawn on a bank other than the nominated bank) and/or documents under a complying presentation, by advancing or agreeing to advance funds to the beneficiary on or before the banking day on which reimbursement is due to the nominated bank.

Sight negotiation credit will nominate the negotiating bank to effect negotiation under the credit, unless the credit is freely negotiable by any bank. This kind of credit enables the beneficiary to get immediate funds from the negotiating bank by presenting to that bank the documents required by the credit including a sight draft. In paying the beneficiary, the negotiating bank retains the right of recourse to the beneficiary if the issuing bank fails to take up the documents.

Sight L/C is beneficial to the exporter since he can get immediate payment.

(b) Usance L/C

—Negotiation documentary credit with a usance draft

This credit requires a usance draft and will nominate negotiating bank to effect negotiation unless the credit is freely negotiable. The negotiating bank will process the documents presented to it and forward them to the issuing bank at maturity.

However, the negotiating bank may purchase the draft and pay the beneficiary the discounted proceeds (the face amount less interest for the usance period), with right of recourse to him if the issuing bank fails to take up the documents. When the usance draft falls due, the negotiating bank will claim reimbursement from the reimbursing bank.

—Acceptance documentary credit

Acceptance documentary credit will nominate the accepting bank to effect acceptance under the credit on presentation of the required documents including a usance draft. By nominating the accepting bank, the issuing bank authorizes this bank to accept the draft under the credit, and undertakes to reimburse the bank at maturity. The beneficiary presents the documents and usance draft to the accepting bank which will then accept the draft and forward the documents to the issuing bank. The accepting bank may then discount the usance draft and pay the beneficiary the discounted proceeds.

—Deferred payment credit

A deferred payment credit is similar to sight payment documentary credit except that the paying bank will pay on a fixed or determinable future date. By nominating the paying bank, the issuing bank authorizes this bank to effect payment at a fixed or determinable time and undertakes to reimburse it on the due date. In this case, the beneficiary will present documents to the paying bank and the bank will settle at the stipulated date. The documents will, then, be passed by the paying bank to the issuing bank. A draft is not essential for this credit, so discounting is not available. However, the exporter can use the credit as collateral to borrow in order to apply for a loan as a pre-shipment financing method.

(c) Usance L/C payable at sight

—Background

When the issuing bank is unable to advance payment, and the importer is unable to pay before taking and selling out the goods, the Usance L/C payable at sight will be in use.

—Features

For Usance L/C payable at sight, the bank discounts the usance draft drawn by the exporter, while the discounting charges are borne by the importer.

—Advantages to buyer and seller

On one hand, Usance L/C payable at sight solves the problem of temporary shortage of funds for the importer; on the other hand, it enables the exporter to get payment immediately.

Comparison with sight L/C:

	Usance L/C payable at sight	Sight L/C
汇票期限	Time draft	Sight draft
票据行为	Presentation, acceptance, discount	Presentation, payment
追索权	The discounter has the right of recourse to the beneficiary	The paying bank does not have the right of recourse to the beneficiary
买方付款赎单期限	Payment at future time	Payment at sight

The similarity between Usance L/C payable at sigh and sight L/C is that the seller gets the face amount of draft immediately.

Comparison with time L/C:

	Usance L/C payable at sight	Time L/C
汇票期限	Time draft	Time draft
票据行为	Presentation, acceptance, discount	Presentation, acceptance, payment
贴现费	Borne by the importer	Borne by the exporter
卖方结汇期限	Getting full payment at sight	Getting payment at future time

(3) Transferable L/C

There are two beneficiaries in a transferable credit. The first beneficiary (exporter) authorizes the advising bank or negotiating bank to transfer the right of issuing a draft in whole to the second beneficiary (supplier). It is the second beneficiary who draws the draft, presents the documents and gets the payment. However, the first beneficiary still undertakes the responsibility of the seller stipulated in the sales contract. A transferable credit can only be transferred once, and the second beneficiary can not transfer it again.

(4) Revolving L/C

If a contract allows for partial shipments, the buyer often requires to establish a revolving credit. It notifies the seller that when a shipment has been made and documents presented and paid, the credit will automatically become re-available and another shipment can be made and so on. The revolving credit can be used again and again until the stipulated total amount have been reached. It simplifies formalities and reduces expenses.

(5) Back-to-back L/C(背对背信用证)

In a back-to-back credit, there are two credits involved. One is issued by the importer's bank in favor of the exporter who is not the actual supplier of goods, the other is issued by the exporter's bank in favor of the actual supplier. The amount of the second credit is less than that in the first credit, the difference being the profit the exporter makes. The tenor is often reduced by a few days to arrange for the substitution of invoices.

Question: What is the difference between transferable credit and back-to-back credit?

(6) Red- clause L/C(红条款信用证)

A red-clause credit is similar to an ordinary credit except that it contains a clause originally typed or printed in red authorizing the negotiating bank to make clean advance to the exporter. Nowadays red-clause credit is mainly used in situations where the importer has an agent in the exporting country whose role is to purchase merchandise to be exported.

Advantages and disadvantages:

(a) For the buyer

—Useful in situations where the buyer trusts the seller and has very high demand for importing the goods.

—But facing the risks of the seller's default of shipment and therefore losing his advance payment.

(b) For the seller

—Getting financing from the buyer.

—But maybe high costs for the financing.

(7) Credit by negotiation, credit by payment and credit by acceptance

The following table shows the differences among the three credits.

	Credit by negotiation	Credit by payment	Credit by acceptance
The bank that makes payment	Negotiation bank	Paying bank	Accepting bank
Right of recourse to the beneficiary(yes/no)	Yes	No	No
Necessity of draft	Draft is essential	Draft is not essential	Draft is not essential

8.3.3.7 Financing methods to both parties under L/C

To seller:

借钱备货

——packing loan

——red clause L/C

交单就收款

—— 出口押汇 / negotiation

承兑就收款

────出口贴现
　　　双保险
　　　　　　──confirmed L/C
To buyer：
　　　远水解得了近渴
　　　　　　　　──usance L/C payable at sight
　　　提单未到不用愁
　　　　　　──T/R

8.3.3.8　Combination of collection with L/C

不可撤销信用证与跟单托收相结合的支付方式,是指部分货款采用信用证支付,部分余额货款采用跟单托收结算。一般的做法,在信用证中应规定出口商须签发两张汇票,一张汇票是依信用证项下部分,货款凭光票付款。另一张汇票须附全部规定的单据,按即期或远期托收。但在信用证中列明如下条款,以示明确。

货款50％应开具不可撤销信用证,其余额50％见票付款交单,全套货运单据应附在托收部分项下。于到期时全数付清发票金额后方可交单。

50％ of the value of goods by irrevocable letter of credit and remaining 50％ on collection basis at sight, the full set of shipping documents are to accompany the collection item. All the documents are not to be delivered to buyer until full payment of the invoice value.

采用不可撤销信用证与跟单托收相结合的支付方式,其优点是：

对进口商来讲,可减少开证保证金,用少数的资金可做大于投资几倍的贸易额,有利于资金的周转,而且可节约银行费用。

对出口商来讲,采用部分使用信用证、部分托收,虽然托收部分须承担一定的风险,但以信用证作保证,这是一种保全的办法。除此之外,还有保全措施,即全部货运单据须附在托收汇票项下,开证银行或付款银行收到单据与汇票时,由银行把住关口,须由进口商全部付清货款后才可把提单交给进口商,以策安全收汇,可防止进口商于信用证项下部分货款付款后,取走提单。

在买卖契约中,开证申请书中及信用证中必须载明,进口商必须付清发票全部金额,才能取得单据。若不付清发票全部金额则装运单据须由银行控制,并凭出口商旨意,予以办理。在信用证上,表示上述功能的文句如下：

兹开立本信用证规定50％发票金额凭即期光票支付,余50％即期付款交单。100％发票金额的全套装运单据随附于托收项下,于进口商付清发票全部金额后交单。若进口方不付清全部金额,则装运单由开证银行(或付款银行)控制,凭出口商旨意予以办理。

We hereby issue this credit stipulating that 50% of the invoice value is available against clean draft at sight while the remaining 50% of documents be held against payment at sight under this credit. The full set of the shipping documents of 100% invoice value shall accompany the collection item and shall only be released after full payment of the invoice value. If the importer fails to pay full invoice value, the shipping documents shall be held by the issuing bank (or paying bank) at the seller's disposal.

UCP600 – Article 38　Transferable Credits

　　a. A bank is under no obligation to transfer a credit except to the extent in the manner expressly consented to by that bank.

　　b. For the purpose of this article:

Transferable credit means a credit that specifically states it is "transferable". A transferable credit may be made available in whole in part to another beneficiary ("second beneficiary") at the request of the beneficiary ("first beneficiary").

Transferring bank means a nominated bank that transfers the credit in a credit available with any bank a bank that is specifically authorized by the issuing bank to transfer that transfers the credit. An issuing bank may be a transferring bank.

Transferred credit means a credit that has been made available by the transferring bank to a second beneficiary.

　　c. Unless otherwise agreed at the time of transfer all charges (such as commissions, fees, costs, expenses) incurred in respect of a transfer must be paid by the first beneficiary.

　　d. A credit may be transferred in part to more than one second beneficiary provided partial drawings shipments are allowed.

A transferred credit can not be transferred at the request of a second beneficiary to any subsequent beneficiary. The first beneficiary is not considered to be a subsequent beneficiary.

　　e. Any request for transfer must indicate if under what conditions

Chapter 8 Payment

amendments may be advised to the second beneficiary. The transferred credit must clearly indicate those conditions.

f. If a credit is transferred to more than one second beneficiary, rejection of an amendment by one or more second beneficiary does not invalidate the acceptance by any other second beneficiary, with respect to which the transferred credit will be amended accordingly. For any second beneficiary that rejected the amendment, the transferred credit will remain un-amended.

g. The transferred credit must accurately reflect the terms conditions of the credit including confirmation if any with the exception of:

— the amount of the credit

— any unit price stated therein

— the expiry date

— the period for presentation or

— the latest shipment date given period for shipment, any or all of which may be reduced or curtailed.

The percentage for which insurance cover must be effected may be increased to provide the amount of cover stipulated in the credit or these articles.

The name of the first beneficiary may be substituted for that of the applicant in the credit.

If the name of the applicant is specifically required by the credit to appear in any document other than the invoice, such requirement must be reflected in the transferred credit.

h. The first beneficiary has the right to substitute its own invoice draft, if any, for those of a second beneficiary for an amount not in excess of that stipulated in the credit, and upon such substitution the first beneficiary can draw under the credit for the difference, if any, between its invoice and the invoice of a second beneficiary.

i. If the first beneficiary is to present its own invoice draft if any but fails to do so on first demand, or if the invoices presented by the first beneficiary create discrepancies that did not exist in the presentation made by the second beneficiary, the first beneficiary fails to correct them on first demand, the transferring bank has the right to present the documents as received the second beneficiary to the issuing bank without further responsibility to the first beneficiary.

j. The first beneficiary, may, in its request for transfer, indicate that honour negotiation is to be effected to a second beneficiary at the place to which the credit has been transferred, up to including the expiry date of the credit. This is without prejudice to the right of the first beneficiary in accordance with sub-article 38 (h).

k. Presentation of documents by or on behalf of a second beneficiary must be made to the transferring bank.

UCP600 第 38 条　可转让信用证

a. 银行无办理信用证转让的义务,除非其明确同意。

b. 就本条而言:

可转让信用证系指特别注明"可转让(transferable)"字样的信用证。可转让信用证可应受益人(第一受益人)的要求转为全部或部分由另一受益人(第二受益人)兑用。

转让行系指办理信用证转让的指定银行,或当信用证规定可在任何银行兑用时,指开证行特别如此授权并实际办理转让的银行。开证行也可担任转让行。

已转让信用证指已由转让行转为可由第二受益人兑用的信用证。

c. 除非转让时另有约定,有关转让的所有费用(诸如佣金、手续费,成本或开支)须由第一受益人支付。

d. 只要信用证允许部分支款或部分发运,信用证可以分部分转让给数名第二受益人。

已转让信用证不得应第二受益人的要求转让给任何其后受益人。第一受益人不视为其后受益人。

e. 任何转让要求须说明是否允许及在何条件下允许将修改通知第二受益人。已转让信用证须明确说明该项条件。

f. 如果信用证转让给数名第二受益人,其中一名或多名第二受益人对信用证的修改并不影响其他第二受益人接受修改。对接受者而言,该已转让信用证即被相应修改,而对拒绝修改的第二受益人而言,该信用证未被修改。

g. 已转让信用证须准确转载原证条款,包括保兑(如果有的话),但下列项目除外:

— 信用证金额

— 规定的任何单价

— 截止日

— 交单期限,或

—最迟发运日或发运期间。

以上任何一项或全部均可减少或缩短。

必须投保的保险比例可以增加,以达到原信用证或本惯例规定的保险金额。

可用第一受益人的名称替换原证中的开证申请人名称。

如果原证特别要求开证申请人名称应在除发票以外的任何单据出现时,已转让信用证必须反映该项要求。

h. 第一受益人有权以自己的发票和汇票(如有的话)替换第二受益人的发票和汇票,其金额不得超过原信用证的金额。经过替换后,第一受益人可在原信用证项下支取自己发票与第二受益人发票间的差价(如有的话)。

i. 如果第一受益人应提交自己的发票和汇票(如有的话),但未能按第一次要求的照办,或第一受益人提交的发票导致了第二受益人的交单中本不存在的不符点,而其未能在第一次要求时修正,转让行有权将从第二受益人处收到的单据照交开证行,并不再对第一受益人承担责任。

j. 在要求转让时,第一受益人可以要求在信用证转让后的兑用地点,在原信用证的截止日之前(包括截止日),对第二受益人承付或议付。该规定并不得损害第一受益人在第 38 条 h 款下的权利。

k. 第二受益人或代表第二受益人的交单必须交给转让行。

Exercise

Ⅰ. Multiple choice

1. 在托收项下,单据的编制通常以(　　)为依据。如有特殊要求,应参照相应的文件或资料。
   A. 信用证　　　　B. 发票　　　　C. 合同　　　　D. 提单

2. 信用证经保兑后,保兑行(　　)。
   A. 只有在开证行没有能力付款时,才承担保证付款的责任
   B. 和开证行一样,承担第一性的付款责任
   C. 需和开证行商议决定双方各自的责任
   D. 只有在买方没有能力付款时,才承担保证付款的责任

3. 信用证的有效期为 1 个月,6 个月或者类似规定,但没有注明从什么时候开始,按照《UCP600》规定,其起算日应该从(　　)。
   A. 申请开证日期开始　　B. 开立信用证日期开始　　C. 通知信用证日期开始

4. 有出口商签发的要求银行在一定时间内付款的汇票不可能是(　　)。

A. 商业汇票   B. 银行汇票   C. 远期汇票

5. 有出口商签发的要求银行在一定时间内付款并经付款人承兑的汇票(   )。

   A. 既是商业汇票又是银行承兑汇票   B. 既是银行汇票又是远期汇票

   C. 既是商业汇票又是银行汇票

6. 在下列有关可转让信用证的说明中,错误的是(   )。

   A. 该证的第一受益人可以将信用证转让给一个或一个以上的人使用

   B. 该证的第二受益人不得再次转让

   C. 该证转让后由第二受益人对合同履行负责

7. 我某进口公司与国外某公司达成一笔进口交易,合同规定通过中国银行开立的不可撤销.可转让的信用证,信用证内对转让费的负担未作规定,按《UCP600》规定,此项费用由(   )。

   A. 我进口公司负担   B. 第一受益人负担   C. 第二受益人负担

8. 保兑信用证的保兑行,责任是(   )。

   A. 在开证行不履行付款义务时履行付款义务

   B. 在开证申请人不履行付款义务时履行付款义务

   C. 承担第一性的付款义务

9. 假远期信用证,就出口商的收汇时间来说等于(   )。

   A. 即期信用证   B. 远期信用证   C. 备用信用证

10. 托收.信用证使用的汇票都是商业汇票,都是通过银行收款,则(   )。

   A. 两者都属于商业信用

   B. 两者都属于银行信用

   C. 托收是商业信用,信用证是银行信用

11. 在国际货款支付中,托收是商业信用,信用证是银行信用,因此(   )。

   A. 两者使用的汇票都是商业汇票

   B. 两者使用的汇票都是银行汇票

   C. 托收使用商业汇票,信用证是银行汇票

12. 买卖双方以 D/P·T/R 条件签订合同,货到目的地后,买方凭 T/R 向代收行借单提货,事后收不回货款(   )。

   A. 代收行应负责向卖方偿付

   B. 由卖方自行负担

   C. 由卖方与代收行协商共同负担

13. 在一笔出口业务中,付款方式采用信用证和 D/P 即期各半,为收汇安全,应在合同中规定(   )。

   A. 开两张汇票,各随附一套等价的货运单据

B. 开两张汇票,信用证下采用光票,托收下使用跟单汇票

C. 开两张汇票,信用证下采用跟单汇票,托收下使用光票

14. 信用证开理的基础是买卖合同,又是开证行对受益人的有条件的付款承诺,所以,但凡信用证条款与买卖合同规定不一致时,受益人可以要求( )。

   A. 开证行修改　　　　B. 开证申请人修改　　　　C. 通知行修改

15. 一张金额为 10 万美元的可撤销信用证,未规定是否分批装运,受益人装出价值为 5 万美元的货物,将单据交议付行议付的第二天,受到开证行撤销该信用证的通知,此时,开证行( )。

   A. 对已经议付的 5 万元,仍应该偿付,其余的立即失效

   B. 对已经议付的 5 万元,拒绝偿付,并且指示议付行追索已经议付的 5 万元

   C. 因撤销通知到达前已经部分议付,故本证仍然全部有效

16. 托收方式下 D/P 和 D/A 的主要区别( )。

   A. D/P 属于跟单托收,D/A 属于光票托收

   B. D/P 属于付款后交单,D/A 属于承兑交单

   C. D/P 为即期付款,D/A 为远期付款

17. 使用 L/C、D/P 和 D/A 三种支付方式结算货款,就卖方的收汇风险而言,从小到大以此排序( )。

   A. D/P、D/A 和 L/C

   B. D/A、D/P 和 L/C

   C. L/C、D/P 和 D/A

18. 信用证规定有效期为 2009 年 11 月 30 日,而没有规定装运期,则可理解为( )。

   A. 最迟装运期为 2009 年 11 月 1 日

   B. 最迟装运期为 2009 年 11 月 15 日

   C. 最迟装运期为 2009 年 11 月 30 日

19. 本票和汇票的区别主要是( )。

   A. 本票是书面支付承诺,汇票是书面支付命令

   B. 本票的付款人是银行,汇票的付款人都是工商企业

   C. 本票都是即期的,汇票有即期和远期的

   D. 本票的票面有两个当事人,汇票是三个当事人

   E. 远期本票不需承兑,远期汇票要承兑

20. 按 CIF 成交的合同,卖方交货后办理交单议付,必须提交的单据包括( )。

   A. 商业发票　　　　B. 保险单　　　　C. 提单

   D. 商检证书　　　　E. 产地证书

21. 假远期信用证又称为买方远期信用证,主要特点是( )。

A. 由开证行开出延期付款的信用证　　　B. 由受益人开出远期汇票
C. 由指定的付款行负责贴现汇票　　　　D. 由进口人负担贴现和费用
E. 由出口人待汇票到期时收回货款

22. 根据《UCP600》规定，必须规定交单地点的信用证是（　　）。
　　A. 即期付款信用证　　　B. 延期付款信用证　　　C. 承兑信用证
　　D. 自由议付信用证　　　E. 限制议付信用证

23. 进出口业务中，使用的商业发票是（　　）。
　　A. 卖方开立的关于货物的清单
　　B. 出口地银行向进口地银行签发的结汇凭证
　　C. 买卖双方交接货物和结算货款的主要单证
　　D. 进出口报关完税的单证
　　E. 买方向卖方索赔的单证

24. 《UCP600》规定，可转让信用证是（　　）。
　　A. 信用证中应该注明可转让
　　B. 可转让信用证只能转让一次
　　C. 第二受益人可以把信用证再转让给第一受益人
　　D. 转让费用应该由第一受益人负担
　　E. 信用证只能按原证规定转让，其他条款不得变更

25. 某银行签发一张汇票，以另一家银行为受票人，则这张汇票是（　　）。
　　A. 商业汇票　　　　　　B. 银行汇票
　　C. 商业承兑汇票　　　　D. 银行承兑汇票

26. 某公司签发一张汇票，上面注明"At 90 days after sight"，则这是一张（　　）。
　　A. 即期汇票　　　B. 远期汇票　　　C. 光票　　　D. 跟单汇票

27. 属于汇票必要项目的是（　　）。
　　A. "付一不付二"的注明　　　B. 付款时间
　　C. 对价条款　　　　　　　　D. 禁止转让的文字

28. 计算汇票付款具体时间时，必须包括（　　）。
　　A. 见票日　　　B. 出票日　　　C. 提单日　　　D. 付款日

29. 在汇票的使用过程中，使汇票一切债务终止的环节是（　　）。
　　A. 提示　　　B. 承兑　　　C. 背书　　　D. 付款

30. 承兑人对出票人指示不加限制地同意确认，这是（　　）。
　　A. 一般承兑　　　B. 特别承兑　　　C. 普通承兑　　　D. 限制承兑

31. 持票人将汇票提交付款人的行为是（　　）。
　　A. 提示　　　B. 承兑　　　C. 背书　　　D. 退票

32. 如果出票人想避免承担被追索的责任,也可以在汇票上加注(   )。
    A. 付一不付二   B. 见索即偿   C. 不受追索   D. 单到付款
33. 背书人在汇款背面只有签名,不写背书人,这是(   )。
    A. 限定性背书   B. 特别背书   C. 记名背书   D. 空白背书
34. 在信用证结算方式下,汇票的受款人通常的抬头方式是(   )。
    A. 限制性抬头   B. 指示性抬头   C. 持票人抬头   D. 来人抬头
35. 在我国实际出口业务中,出口公司开出的汇票在信用证结算方式下出票条款应填写(   )。
    A. 合同号码及签订日期   B. 发票号码及签发日期
    C. 提单号码及签发日期   D. 信用证号码及出证日期
36. 某支票签发人在银行的存款总额低于他所签发的支票票面金额,他签发这种支票称(   )。
    A. 现金支票   B. 转帐支票   C. 旅行支票   D. 空头支票
37. 属于顺汇方法的支付方式是(   )。
    A. 汇付   B. 托收   C. 信用证   D. 银行保函
38. 接受汇出行的委托将款项解付给收款人的银行是(   )。
    A. 托收银行   B. 汇入行   C. 代收行   D. 转递行
39. 属于汇付活动当事人的是(   )。
    A. 委托人   B. 汇出行   C. 解付行   D. 索偿行
40. 通过汇出行开立的银行汇票的转移实现货款支付的汇付方式是(   )。
    A. 电汇   B. 信汇   C. 票汇   D. 银行转帐
41. T/T 是指(   )。
    A. 提单   B. 电汇   C. 信用证   D. 远期汇款
42. 在汇付方式中,能为收款人提供融资便利的方式是(   )。
    A. 信汇   B. 票汇   C. 电汇   D. 远期汇款
43. 属于银行信用的国际贸易的支付方式是(   )。
    A. 汇付   B. 托收   C. 信用证   D. 票汇
44. 在托收结算方式下,一旦货款被买方拒付,在进口地承担货物的提货、报关、存仓、转售等责任的当事人是(   )。
    A. 委托人   B. 托收银行   C. 代收银行   D. 付款人
45. D/P·T/R 意指(   )。
    A. 付款交单   B. 承兑交单
    C. 付款交单凭信托收据借单   D. 承兑交单凭信托收据借单
46. 承兑交单方式下开立的汇票是(   )。

A. 即期汇票　　　B. 远期汇票　　　C. 银行汇票　　　D. 银行承兑汇票

47. 在国际贸易中,用以统一解释、调和信用证各有关当事人矛盾的国际惯例是(　　)。
   A.《托收统一规则》　　　　　B.《国际商会 600 号出版物》
   C.《合约保证书同意规则》　　 D. 以上答案都不对

48. 信用证支付方式实际上把进口人履行的付款责任转移给(　　)。
   A. 出口人　　　B. 银行　　　C. 供货商　　　D. 最终用户

49. 在信用证方式下,银行保证向信用证受益人履行付款责任的条件是(　　)。
   A. 受益人按期履行合同　　　　　B. 受益人按信用证规定交货
   C. 受益人提交严格符合信用证要求的单据　　D. 开证申请人付款赎单

50. 对于信用证与合同关系的表述正确的是(　　)。
   A. 信用证的开立以买卖合同为依据
   B. 信用证的履行不受买卖合同的约束
   C. 有关银行只根据信用证的规定办理信用证业务
   D. 合同是审核信用证的依据

Ⅱ. True or false statements.

1. 我某公司按 CIF 条件出口某商品,采用信用证支付方式,买方在约定时间内未开来信用证,但约定的装运期已到,为了重合同和守信用,我方仍应按期发运货物。(　　)

2. 汇票、本票、支票都可分为即期和远期两种。(　　)

3. 信用证支付方式是属于银行信用,所使用的汇票是银行汇票。(　　)

4. 托收的支付方式是属于商业信用,所使用的汇票是商业汇票。(　　)

5. 在票汇的情况下,买方购买银行汇票径寄卖方,因为采用的是银行汇票,故这种付款方式属于银行信用。(　　)

6. 国外开来信用证规定货物数量为 3000 箱,6/7/8 月份,每月平均装运,我出口公司于 6 月份装运 1000 箱,并收妥款项。7 月份由于货未备妥,未能装运,8 月份装运 2000 箱,根据《UCP600》规定,银行不得拒付。(　　)

7. 在信用证支付方式下,受益人只要在信用证规定的有效期内向银行提交符合信用证规定的全部单据,银行就必须履行付款义务。(　　)

8. 根据《UCP600》规定,一切信用证均需规定一个付款、承兑和议付的交单地点。(　　)

9. 如果受益人要求开证申请人将信用证的有效期延长一个月,在信用证未规定装运期的情况下,同一信用证上的装运期也可以顺延一个月。(　　)

10. 信用证修改通知有多项内容时,只能全部接受或全部拒绝。(　　)
11. 根据《UCP600》规定,可转让信用证只能转让一次,但是第二受益人将信用证再次转让给第一受益人,不属于被禁止转让的范围。(　　)
12. 可转让信用证办理转让后,买卖合同也随之由第一受益人转让给第二受益人。(　　)
13. 一张不可撤销信用证列有装运期,而没有列有效期,根据《UCP600》规定,受益人应该在最后装运期前向银行交单。(　　)
14. D/A 30 天付款比 D/P 30 天付款对出口商来说承担的风险更大。(　　)
15. 付款交单和承兑交单对卖方来说都有一定风险,但是承兑交单最容易被买方接受,有利于达成交易,所以在进出口合同中,应该扩大对承兑交单的使用。(　　)
16. 银行汇票和商业汇票的主要区别在于:前者的出票人、付款人都是银行,后者的出票人、付款人都是工商企业。(　　)
17. 买方使用假远期信用证,主要是为了利用第三国银行的资金。(　　)
18. 延期付款和分期付款都是买方利用外资的一种形式。(　　)
19. 可撤销信用证对出口人安全收汇没有保障,因为开证行可以在任何情况下单方面撤销和修改信用证。(　　)
20. 国外开来信用证规定最迟装运期为 4 月 30 日,有效期为 5 月 15 日,我外贸公司在 4 月 12 日将货物装船并取得提单,在 5 月 6 日向议付行提交符合信用证规定的单据,按《UCP600》规定,银行应该予以议付。(　)

Ⅲ. Term definition

1. 信用证
2. 循环信用证
3. 承兑交单
4. 汇票
5. 本票
6. 电汇
7. 不可撤销信用证

Ⅳ. Case study

1. 某出口企业收到一份国外开来的不可撤销的即期议付信用证,正准备按信用证规定发运货物时,突接开证银行通知,声称开证申请人已经倒闭。对此,出口企业应如何处理? 依据何在?
2. 我国某公司与某外商签定一份以信用证方式支付的 CIF 出口合同。对方来证规定:装运期不得迟于8月5日,信用证有效期为8月31日。我公司于8月28日向议付行提交签发日期为8月5日的提单,却遭到议付行拒付。请问议付行拒付有无道理,为什么?

3. 青岛某公司以CIF为条件对外出口一批货物,买方开来了保兑信用证。该信用证规定:银行收到符合要求的单据后付款90%,余下的10%须等货物到达目的地后,买方通知银行方可支付。当货轮到达目的港外海时,接当地港务局通知,因目的港拥挤,货轮在该港的辅助港卸货。于是,买方以货物未在约定港口卸货为由,拒付余额货款。请问:

(1)买方拒付的理由是否合理,为什么?

(2)出口方能否要求付款行及保兑行付款?

(3)从本案中应吸取什么教训?

4. 我国某公司向外国某商进口一批钢材,货物分两批装运,支付方式为不可撤销即期信用证,每批分别由中国银行开立一份信用证。第一批货物装运后,卖方在有效期内向银行对议付行作了偿付。我方在收到第一批货物后,发现货物品质不符合同,因而要求开证行对第二份信用证项下的单据拒绝付款,但遭到开证行拒绝。你认为开证行这样做是否合理?

Ⅴ. Review L/C

Sample of L/C:

Issue of a Documentary Credit		
Issuing Bank:		BKJPYUTYA08E SESSION: 000 ISN: 000000 BANK OF NEWYORK, OSAKA NO.216 ,AUMAHU, AKI_GUN, OSAKA,JAPAN
Destination Bank:		BANK OF CHINA,WENZHOU BRANCH 153, RENMING RD WENZHOU CHINA TEL:0577-86689999
Type of Documentary Credit	40A	IRREVOCABLE
Credit Number	20	LGU-002156
Date of Issue	31G	20080402
Date and Place of Expiry	31D	20080630,CHINA

Applicant	50	YOUNGAN TRADING CO., 163,KUMI RD.,OSAKA
Beneficiary	59	JIAHA INTER TRADING CO., 60, CHEZHAN RD WENZHOU ZHEJIANG,CHINA
Currency Code, Amount	32B	USD 26,520.00
Available with...by...	41D	ANY BANK BY NEGOTIATION
Drafts at	42C	AT SIGHT
Drawee	42D	NEWYORK BANK,OSAKA
Partial Shipments	43P	NOT ALLOWED
Transshipment	43T	NOT ALLOWED

Shipping on Board/Dispatch/Packing in Charge at/ from

44A SHANGHAI

Transportation to	44B	OSAKA,JAPAN
Latest Date of Shipment	44C	20080615

Description of Goods or Services: 45A

100PCT RAYON DIASH CLOTH

30S×30S/56×54/40×40CM 2PLY

CIF OSAKA

CHINA ORIGIN

Documents Required: 46A

1. SIGNED COMMERCIAL INVOICE IN 5 COPIES.
2. FULL SET OF CLEAN ON BOARD OCEAN BILLS OF LADING MADE OUT TO ORDER AND BLANK ENDORSED, MARKED "FREIGHT PREPAID" NOTIFYING ACCOUNTEE.
3. PACKING LIST/WEIGHT MEMO IN 4 COPIES INDICATING QUANTITY/GROSS AND NET WEIGHTS OF EACH PACKAGE AND PACKING CONDITIONS AS CALLED FOR BY THE L/C.
4. CERTIFICATE OF QUALITY IN 3 COPIES ISSUED BY PUBLIC RECOGNIZED SURVEYOR.
5. BENEFICIARY'S CERTIFIED COPY OF FAX DISPATCHED TO THE ACCOUNTEE WITH 3 DAYS AFTER SHIPMENT ADVISING NAME OF VESSEL, DATE, QUANTITY, WEIGHT, VALUE OF SHIPMENT, L/C NUMBER AND CONTRACT NUMBER.

6. CERTIFICATE OF ORIGIN IN 3 COPIES ISSUED BY AUTHORIZED INSTITUTION.
7. CERTIFICATE OF HEALTH IN 3 COPIES ISSUED BY AUTHORIZED INSTITUTION.

ADDITIONAL INSTRUCTIONS: 47A

1. CHARTER PARTY B/L AND THIRD PARTY DOCUMENTS ARE ACCEPTABLE.
2. SHIPMENT PRIOR TO L/C ISSUING DATE IS ACCEPTABLE.
3. BOTH QUANTITY AND AMOUNT 10 PERCENT MORE OR LESS ARE ALLOWED.

Charges	71B	ALL BANKING CHARGES OUTSIDE THE OPENNING BANK ARE FOR BENEFICIARY'S ACCOUNT.
Period for Presentation	48	DOCUMENTS MUST BE PRESENTED WITHIN 15 DAYS AFTER THE DATE OF ISSUANCE OF THE TRANSPORT DOCUMENTS BUT WITHIN THE VALIDITY OF THE CREDIT.
Confirmation Instructions	49	WITHOUT

Instructions to the Paying/Accepting/Negotiating Bank: 78

1. ALL DOCUMENTS TO BE FORWARDED IN ONE COVER, UNLESS OTHERWISE STATED ABOVE.
2. DISCREPANT DOCUMENT FEE OF USD 50.00 OR EQUAL CURRENCY WILL BE DEDUCTED FROM DRAWING IF DOCUMENTS WITH DISCREPANCIES ARE ACCEPTED.

"Advising Through" Bank	57A	BANK OF CHINA, WENZHOU BRANCH 153 RENMING RD WENZHOU, CHINA TEL: 0577-86689999

********other wordings between banks are omitted********

Assignment：

(1)找出信用证的主要当事人并分析相互的业务关系：申请人、受益人、开证行、议付行、通知行。

(2)找出信用证的到期地点。

(3)找出信用证的到期日。

(4)找出信用证的交单时间。

(5)分析本信用证是即期还是远期信用证。

(6)找出信用证对货物运输的要求(目的港、出发港、装运时间要求)。

(7)找出信用证中货物的描述部分，标出出口货物名称。

(8)找出信用证描述单据要求的部分，指出需要提交的单据种数。

(9)找出信用证对议付行的要求。

(10)对照已经学习过的信用证种类，总结出本信用证的种类。

Chapter 9　Documents

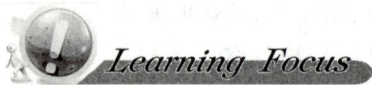

Commercial invoice
Certificate of origin form A
Ocean bill of lading
Insurance policy

Documents are at the heart of all forms of international payment, especially documentary credits. Documents are of great importance to all parties to the transaction. Any small changes in wording can mean a successful or unsuccessful transaction.

9.1　Commercial Invoice

Major functions:
The certificate of the buyer for his performance of the contract.
A condition on which the bank makes payment.
Basis for preparing insurance policy, transport documents or other documents.

Cautions and notes:
(1) Description of goods in invoice must precisely comply with that in L/C.
(2) Invoice amount and currency should match exactly those in L/C.
(3) Unless otherwise stipulated, the invoice must be made out in the name of the applicant or buyer.
(4) The buyer, seller and banks should all carefully check for discrepancies in the invoice.

A sample of commercial invoice:

ZHEJIANG TEXITLES IMPORT AND EXPORT CO. ,LTD(1)

COMMERCIAL INVOICE(2)

TO:(3)	NO. :(4)		
	DATE:(5)		
	S/C NO. :(6)		
	L/C NO. :(7)		
FROM TO (8)			
MARKS & NOS(9)	DESCRIPTIONS OF GOODS KIND & NUMBER OF PACKAGE(10)	QUANTITY (11)	UNIT PRICE(12)	AMOUNT (13)

TOTAL AMOUNT: (14)
PACKING IN   (15)

商业发票编制说明：

(1)出票人名称与地址(出口公司)

(2)发票名称

(3)发票抬头人名称与地址(信用证方式下的指定抬头人,托收方式下合同买方的名称和地址)

(4)发票号码

(5)发票日期

(6)合同号码

(7)信用证号码

(8)运输资料

(9)唛头及件号

(10)货物描述

(11)数量

(12)单价

(13)总金额

9.2　Certificate of Origin Form A

Certificate of Origin Form A is a document required by the customs authorities of many developed nations to prove eligibility of imported goods under duty-free import programs such as the Generalized System of Preferences (GSP).

产地证

①Exporter　(full name, address, country)	Certificate No.			
②Consignee　(full name, address, country)	GENERALIZED SYSTEM OF PREFERANCES CERTIFICATE OF ORIGIN(Combined declaration and certificate)			
③Means of transport and route	④For official use			
⑤Item number	⑥Marks and numbers of packages	⑦Description of goods; Number and kind of packages	⑧ Origin criterion	⑨ Gross weight or other quantity	⑩ Number and date of invoices
⑪Certification It is hereby certified, on the basis of control carried out, that the declaration of the exporter is correct	⑫Declaration by exporter The undersigned hereby declares that the above details and statement are correct; that all goods were produced in CHINA (country) _____ and that they comply with the origin requirements specified for those goods in the Generalized System of Preference for goods exported to (importing country)			

普惠制产地证编制说明：

(1)出口商名称、地址、国家

(2)收货人名称、地址、国家

(3)运输方式及路线

(4)供官方使用

(5)商品顺序号

(6)唛头及包装号

(7)包件数量及种类、商品名称

(8)原产地标准

(9)毛重或其他数量

(10)发票号码及日期

(11)签证当局的证明

(12)出口商的声明

9.3　Ocean Bill of Lading

Ocean bill of lading is a transport document covering port-to-port shipment of goods (for carriage of goods solely by sea).

Key issues:

(1) A negotiable instrument.

(2) The full set of originals is key.

(3) Loaded "On board" notation or shipped on a named vessel is crucial.

(4) A document of title to the good.

Types of ocean bill of lading	Brief explanations
①On board B/L	Also shipped B/L
②Receipt for shipment B/L	Not shipped on board
③Clean B/L	With no qualifying remarks
④Unclean B/L	With such remarks or notations as: "one bag stained by water, one bag broken"
⑤Direct B/L	No transshipment
⑥Transshipment B/L	With transshipment
⑦Linear B/L	Goods shipped by the linear
⑧Charter party B/L	Goods shipped by the vessel rented or chartered
⑨Freight prepaid or paid B/L	Freight prepaid or paid, usually for CIF terms
⑩Freight to collect or payable at destination	Usually used for FOB or FCR terms
⑪Under deck B/L	Goods shipped under deck
⑫On deck B/L	Goods shipped on deck

The sample of ocean bill of lading is shown in Chapter 6.

海运提单编制说明：

(1)托运人

(2)收货人

(3)被通知人

(4)提单号码

(5)前段运输

(6)收货地点

(7)船名航次

(8)装运港

(9)卸货港

(10)最终目的地

(11)唛头、集装箱箱号

(12)件数和包装种类

(13)货物名称及描述

(14)毛重

(15)尺码

(16)特殊条款

(17)运费条款

(18)正本提单份数

(19)提单签发地点及日期

(20)提单的签署

9.4　Insurance Policy

An insurance policy provides actionable evidence of a contract of insurance. It is the evidence that cover has been effected under an open policy. For the sample of insurance policy, please refer to Chapter 7.

保险单编制说明：

(1)保险公司名称

(2)保险单据名称

(3)发票号码

(4)保险单号码

(5)被保险人

Chapter 9　Documents

（6）唛头

（7）包装及数量

（8）货物名称

（9）保险金额

（10）保险费及保险费率

（11）装载运输工具

（12）开航日期

（13）起讫地点

（14）承保险别

（15）赔款偿付地点

（16）日期

（17）签字

（18）其他

（19）份数

UCP 600 – Article 14　Standard for Examination of Documents

　　a. A nominated bank acting on its nomination, a confirming bank, if any, and the issuing bank must examine a presentation to determine, on the basis of the documents alone, whether or not the documents appear on their face to constitute a complying presentation.

　　b. A nominated bank acting on its nomination, a confirming bank, if any, and the issuing bank shall each have a maximum of five banking days following the day of presentation to determine if a presentation is complying. This period is not curtailed or otherwise affected by the occurrence on or after the date of presentation of any expiry date or last day for presentation.

　　c. A presentation including one or more original transport documents subject to articles 19, 20, 21, 22, 23, 24 or 25 must be made by or on behalf of the beneficiary not later than 21 calendar days after the date of shipment as described in these rules, but in any event not later than the expiry date of the credit.

　　d. Data in a document, when read in context with the credit, the document itself and international standard banking practice, need not be identical to, but must not conflict with, data in that document, any other stipulated document or the credit.

e. In documents other than the commercial invoice, the description of the goods, services or performance, if stated, may be in general terms not conflicting with their descriptions in the credit.

f. If a credit requires presentation of a document other than a transport document, insurance document or commercial invoice, without stipulating by whom the document is to be issued or its data content, banks will accept the document as presented if its content appears to fulfill the function of the required document and otherwise complies with sub-article 14 (d).

g. A document presented but not required by the credit will be disregarded and may be returned to the presenter.

h. If a credit contains a condition without stipulating the document to indicate compliance with the condition, banks will deem such condition as not stated and will disregard it.

i. A document may be dated prior to the issuance date of the credit, but must not be dated later than its date of presentation.

j. When the addresses of the beneficiary and the applicant appear in any stipulated document, they need not be the same as those stated in the credit or in any other stipulated document, but must be within the same country as the respective addresses mentioned in the credit. Contact details (telefax, telephone, email and the like) stated as part of the beneficiary's and the applicant's address will be disregarded. However, when the address and contact details of the applicant appear as part of the consignee or notify party details on a transport document subject to articles 19, 20, 21, 22, 23, 24 or 25, they must be as stated in the credit.

k. The shipper or consignor of the goods indicated on any document need not be the beneficiary of the credit.

A transport document may be issued by any party other than a carrier, owner, master or charterer provided that the transport document meets the requirements of articles 19, 20, 21, 22, 23 or 24 of these rules.

UCP 600 第 14 条　审核单据的标准

a. 按照指定行事的被指定银行、保兑行(如有)以及开证行必须对提示的单据进行审核,并仅以单据为基础,以决定单据在表面上看来是否构成相符

Chapter 9　Documents

提示。

　　b. 按照指定行事的被指定银行、保兑行(如有)以及开证行,自其收到提示单据的翌日起算,应各自拥有最多不超过 5 个银行工作日的时间以决定提示是否相符。该期限不因单据提示日适逢信用证有效期或最迟提示期或在其之后而被缩减或受到其他影响。

　　c. 提示若包含一份或多份按照本惯例第 19 条、20 条、21 条、22 条、23 条、24 条或 25 条出具的正本运输单据,则必须由受益人或其代表按照相关条款在不迟于装运日后的 21 个公历日内提交,但无论如何不得迟于信用证的到期日。

　　d. 单据中内容的描述不必与信用证、信用证对该项单据的描述以及国际标准银行实务完全一致,但不得与该项单据中的内容、其他规定的单据或信用证相冲突。

　　e. 除商业发票外,其他单据中的货物、服务或行为描述若须规定,可使用统称,但不得与信用证规定的描述相矛盾。

　　f. 如果信用证要求提示运输单据、保险单据和商业发票以外的单据,但未规定该单据由何人出具或单据的内容。如信用证对此未做规定,只要所提交单据的内容看来满足其功能需要且其他方面与 14 条(d)款相符,银行将对提示的单据予以接受。

　　g. 提示信用证中未要求提交的单据,银行将不予置理。如果收到此类单据,可以退还提示人。

　　h. 如果信用证中包含某项条件而未规定须提交与之相符的单据,银行将认为未列明此条件,并对此不予置理。

　　i. 单据的出单日期可以早于信用证开立日期,但不得迟于信用证规定的提示日期。

　　j. 当受益人和申请人的地址显示在任何规定的单据上时,不必与信用证或其他规定单据中显示的地址相同,但必须与信用证中述及的各自地址处于同一国家内。用于联系的资料(电子传真、电话、电子邮箱及类似方式)如作为受益人和申请人地址的组成部分将被不予置理。然而,当申请人的地址及联系信息作为按照第 19 条、20 条、21 条、22 条、23 条、24 条或 25 条出具的运输单据中收货人或通知方详址的组成部分时,则必须按照信用证规定予以显示。

　　k. 显示在任何单据中的货物的托运人或发货人不必是信用证的受益人。假如运输单据能够满足本惯例第 19 条、20 条、21 条、22 条、23 条或 24 条的要求,则运输单据可以由承运人、船东、船长或租船人以外的任何一方出具。

UCP 600 – Article 33 Hours of Presentation

A bank has no obligation to accept a presentation outside of its banking hours.

UCP 600 第 33 条 交单时间

银行在其营业时间外无接受交单的义务。

UCP 600 – Article 34 Disclaimer on Effectiveness of Documents

A bank assumes no liability or responsibility for the form, sufficiency, accuracy, genuineness, falsification or legal effect of any document, or for the general or particular conditions stipulated in a document or superimposed thereon; nor does it assume any liability or responsibility for the description, quantity, weight, quality, condition, packing, delivery, value or existence of the goods, services or other performance represented by any document, or for the good faith or acts or omissions, solvency, performance or standing of the consignor, the carrier, the forwarder, the consignee or the insurer of the goods or any other person.

UCP 600 第 34 条 关于单据有效性的免责

银行对任何单据的形式、充分性、准确性、内容真实性、虚假性或法律效力，或对单据中规定或添加的一般或特殊条件，概不负责；银行对任何单据所代表的货物、服务或其他履约行为的描述、数量、重量、品质、状况、包装、交付、价值或其存在与否，或对发货人、承运人、货运代理人、收货人、货物的保险人或其他任何人的诚信与否，作为或不作为、清偿能力、履约或资信状况，也概不负责。

Chapter 10 Claims and Arbitration

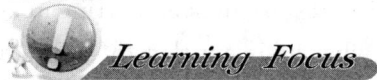

Breach of contract
Claim
Force majeure
Arbitration

10.1 Breach of Contract

10.1.1 Definition of breach of contract

Breach of contract means the refusal or failure by one party to a contract to fulfill an obligation imposed on him under the contract.

10.1.2 Reasons for breach of contract

In international trade, breach of contract is caused by the following situations:

A seller may breach a contract when

(1) He fails to deliver the goods.

(2) He fails to make delivery according to shipment date stipulated in the contract.

(3) He delivers the goods that are not in accordance with the contract of the L/C in terms of quality, quantity, specifications and packing, etc.

(4) He presents shipping documents that are incomplete.

A buyer may breach a contract when

(1) He refuses to accept the goods.
(2) He fails to open the L/C according to the stipulated period.
(3) He fails to dispatch the vessel under FOB contract.

10.1.3 Types of breach of contract

United Nations Convention on Contracts for the International Sale of Goods classifies "breach" into two kinds: fundamental breach and non-fundamental breach. A breach of contract is fundamental if it results in such detriment to the other party as substantially to deprive him of what he is entitled to expect under the contract, unless the party in breach did not foresee and a reasonable person of the same kind in the same circumstance would not have foreseen such a result. If the damage to the other party is not so substantial, then the breach of the contract is non-fundamental.

If a breach of contract is fundamental, then the injured party shall have the right to cancel the contract and recover damages from the party in breach. If a breach of contract is non-fundamental, then the injured party shall have the right to recover damages from the party in breach, but can not cancel the contract.

10.2 Claim

claim 索赔,赔偿,赔偿金
compensate 赔偿,补偿
to make a (one's) claim 提出索赔
to register a (one's) claim 提出索赔
to file a (one's) claim 提出索赔
to lodge a (one's) claim 提出索赔
to raise a (one's) claim 提出索赔
to put in a (one's) claim 提出索赔
to bring up a (one's) claim 提出索赔
to make a claim with (against) sb. 向某方提出索赔
to make a claim for (on) sth. 就某事提出索赔
to waive a claim 放弃索赔

Claim clauses in the sales contract

The following are some typical examples of claim clauses in contract:

(1) In case the quality and/or quantity/weight of the goods found by the buyer are not in conformity with the provisions of the contract after arrival of the goods at the port of destination, the buyer may lodge claim with the seller on such strength of the inspection certificate issued by an inspection organization as is agreed by the parties to the contract, with the exception, however, of the claims for which the insurance company and/or the shipping company are to be held responsible. Claim for quality discrepancy shall, within 30 days after arrival of the goods at the port of destination, be filed by the buyer. While for quantity/weight discrepancy claims shall, within 15 days after arrival of the goods at the port of destination, be filed by the buyer. The seller shall, within 30 days after receipt of the claim requirement, reply to the buyer.

(2) Should the quality, quantity, and/or weight be found not in conformity with those in this contract, aside from those natural changes of quality and weight in transit and losses within the responsibility of the shipping company and/or insurance company, the buyer shall have the right within 30 days after the arrival of the goods at the port of the destination, to lodge claims concerning the quality, quantity or weight of the goods. Claims for perishable goods are to be put forward immediately after arrival of the goods at the destination.

10.3　Force Majeure

10.3.1　Definition of force majeure

Force majeure clause is exempting clause which refers to that a party under a sales contract is exempted for non-fulfillment of his obligations totally or partially as a result of conditions beyond his control, such as earthquake, flood, war, etc.

According to international trade practice, a contract may be suspended or terminated due to a force majeure case. If the performance of contract is only delayed by a force majeure for a short time, the contract may suspend, and the contract should resume after the force majeure incident finishes. However, if the force majeure incident has damaged the basis of the contract, then the contract should terminate.

10.3.2 Force majeure clause in contract

(1) The seller shall not be held responsible for failure or delay to perform all or any part of its obligations specified in the contract due to flood, fire, earthquake, drought, war, or any other events which could not be predicted at the time of the conclusion of the contract, and could not be controlled, avoided or overcome by the seller. Provided that the seller shall, as soon as possible, inform the other party of its occurrence in written form and thereafter send a certificate of the event issued by the relevant authority to the other party thereto within 15 days after its occurrence. If the force majeure event lasts over 20 days, the parties thereto shall negotiate the execution or the termination of the contract.

(2) In case of force majeure, the seller shall not be held responsible for late delivery or non-delivery of the goods, but the buyer shall be notified of this by cable or by fax. The seller should furnish the buyer with a certificate attesting such event(s) if so requested by the Buyer.

(3) The seller shall not be held liable for failure or delay in delivery of the entire lot or a portion of the goods under this sales contract due to any force majeure incidents (Force majure , such as heavy weather, lightning, tsunami, flood,earth quake,fire,explosion,collision and uncontrollable events?)

10.4 Arbitration

In international trade, there are many ways to settle the disputes, namely, friendly negotiation, litigation and arbitration. The most satisfactory way for both parties to settle the dispute is by means of negotiation. However, it is often the case that disputes can not be amicably settled by negotiation. Then it is necessary to resort to arbitration because it brings about a friendly atmosphere and is more flexible, less expensive and much quicker in handling the case than litigation.

10.4.1 Definition of arbitration

Arbitration is a means of settling a dispute between both parties through the medium of a third party who is not partial to either of the parties to the dispute, and whose decision on the dispute is final and binding. Once an arbitral award is made, it has legal binding force and neither party shall appeal for revision before a law court. Compared with litigation, arbitration has a lot of advantages:

The arbitration procedure is simpler and the cost of arbitration is cheaper;

Privacy can be maintained in both the arbitration hearing and the award;

The arbitration award is final and binding upon both parties;

It is less time-consuming in settling the dispute through arbitration.

10.4.2 Arbitration proceedings

(1) Plaintiff's application

The plaintiff shall submit an arbitration application to the arbitration authority which should include the names and address of plaintiff and defendant.

(2) Defendant's defense or counter-charge

After receiving the application, the arbitration authority should ask the defendant to defend himself by the statement of defense. If the defendant wants to make a counter claim, he should lodge a claim within 45 days after receiving the application.

(3) Formation of arbitral tribunal

According to international practice, there are usually three arbitrators, of which two are appointed by the interested parties, while the third arbitrator is appointed by the chairman of the arbitration authority.

(4) The hearings

The arbitral tribunal shall give hearings to the case in accordance with the arbitration rules. The conclusion of the award shall be declared to the parties at the closing session of the hearings.

(5) The award-making

The award is usually final and has the force of law binding upon both parties. The award shall be executed by the parties within the time fixed in the award.

10.4.3 Arbitration clause in contract

An arbitration clause should include such information as place of arbitration, arbitration authority, arbitration rules, effectiveness of award, fees. For example:

Arbitration: All disputes in connection with this contract or the execution thereof shall be settled friendly through negotiations. In case no settlement can be reached, the case may then be submitted for arbitration to China International Economic And Trade Arbitration Commission in accordance with the provisional Rules of Procedures promulgated by the Arbitration Commission. The decision of the Arbitration Commission shall be final and binding upon both parties; neither party shall seek recourse to a law court nor other authorities to appeal for revision of the decision. Arbitration fee shall be borne by the losing party. Or arbitration may be settled in the third country mutually agreed upon by both parties.

Case study：
中国某公司曾与美国某商人签订一项买卖机械设备的合同，合同背面载有仲裁条款。后在履约过程中，双方发生争议，美国商人遂向美国法院起诉中方公司。法院受理此案后，即向中方公司发出传票，中方公司即以合同背面载明的仲裁条款为证，提出抗辩，要求美国法院不予受理，美国法院核实材料后，只好承认它对本案无管辖权。你认为双方应该通过什么途径解决？

The following articles are about the remedies for breach of contract by the seller from *United Nations Convention on Contracts for Sale of Goods*.

第三节　卖方违反合同的补救办法
Section Ⅲ　Remedies for breach of contract by the seller
第 45 条
(1)如果卖方不履行他在合同和本公约中的任何义务，买方可以：
(a)行使第 46 条至第 52 条所规定的权利；
(b)按照第 74 条至第 77 条的规定，要求损害赔偿。
(2)买方可能享有的要求损害赔偿的任何权利，不因他行使采取其他补救办法的权利而丧失。
(3)如果买方对违反合同采取某种补救办法，法院或仲裁庭不得给予卖方宽限期。

Chapter 10 Claims and Arbitration

Article 45

(1) If the seller fails to perform any of his obligations under the contract or this Convention, the buyer may:

(a) Exercise the rights provided in articles 46 to 52;

(b) Claim damages as provided in articles 74 to 77.

(2) The buyer is not deprived of any right he may have to claim damages by exercising his right to other remedies.

(3) No period of grace may be granted to the seller by a court or arbitral tribunal when the buyer resorts to a remedy for breach of contract.

第 46 条

(1)买方可以要求卖方履行义务,除非买方已采取与此要求相抵触的某种补救办法。

(2)如果货物不符合同,买方只有在此种不符合同情形构成根本违反合同时,才可以要求交付替代货物,而且关于替代货物的要求,必须与依照第 39 条发出的通知同时提出,或者在该项通知发出后一段合理时间内提出。

(3)如果货物不符合同,买方可以要求卖方通过修理对不符合同之处做出补救,除非他考虑了所有情况之后,认为这样做是不合理的。修理的要求必须与依照第 39 条发出的通知同时提出,或者在该项通知发出后一段合理时间内提出。

Article 46

(1) The buyer may require performance by the seller of his obligations unless the buyer has resorted to a remedy which is inconsistent with this requirement.

(2) If the goods do not conform with the contract, the buyer may require delivery of substitute goods only if the lack of conformity constitutes a fundamental breach of contract and a request for substitute goods is made either in conjunction with notice given under article 39 or within a reasonable time thereafter.

(3) If the goods do not conform with the contract, the buyer may require the seller to remedy the lack of conformity by repair, unless this is unreasonable having regard to all the circumstances. A request for repair must be made either in conjunction with notice given under article 39 or within a reasonable time thereafter.

第 47 条

(1) 买方可以规定一段合理时限的额外时间,让卖方履行其义务。

(2) 除非买方收到卖方的通知,声称他将不在所规定的时间内履行义务,买方在这段时间内不得对违反合同采取任何补救办法。但是,买方并不因此丧失他对迟延履行义务可能享有的要求损害赔偿的任何权利。

Article 47

(1) The buyer may fix an additional period of time of reasonable length for performance by the seller of his obligations.

(2) Unless the buyer has received notice from the seller that he will not perform within the period so fixed, the buyer may not, during that period, resort to any remedy for breach of contract. However, the buyer is not deprived thereby of any right he may have to claim damages for delay in performance.

第 48 条

(1) 在第 49 条的条件下,卖方即使在交货日期之后,仍可自付费用,对任何不履行义务做出补救,但这种补救不得造成不合理的迟延,也不得使买方遭受不合理的不便,或无法确定卖方是否将偿付买方预付的费用。但是,买方保留本公约所规定的要求损害赔偿的任何权利。

(2) 如果卖方要求买方表明他是否接受卖方履行义务,而买方不在一段合理时间内对此要求做出答复,则卖方可以按其要求中所指明的时间履行义务。买方不得在该段时间内采取与卖方履行义务相抵触的任何补救办法。

(3) 卖方表明他将在某一特定时间内履行义务的通知,应视为包括根据上一款规定要买方表明决定的要求在内。

(4) 卖方按照本条第(2)和第(3)款做出的要求或通知,必须在买方收到后,始生效力。

Article 48

(1) Subject to article 49, the seller may, even after the date for delivery, remedy at his own expense any failure to perform his obligations, if he can do so without unreasonable delay and without causing the buyer unreasonable inconvenience or uncertainty of reimbursement by the seller of expenses advanced by the buyer. However, the buyer retains any right to claim damages as provided for in this convention.

Chapter 10 Claims and Arbitration

(2) If the seller requests the buyer to make known whether he will accept performance and the buyer does not comply with the request within a reasonable time, the seller may perform within the time indicated in his request. The buyer may not, during that period of time, resort to any remedy which is in consistent with performance by the seller.

(3) A notice by the seller that he will perform within a specified period of time is assumed to include a request, under the preceding paragraph, that the buyer make known his decision.

(4) A request or notice by the seller under paragraph (2) or (3) of this article is not effective unless received by the buyer.

第 49 条

(1)买方在以下情况下可以宣告合同无效:
(a)卖方不履行其在合同或本公约中的任何义务,等于根本违反合同;或
(b)如果发生不交货的情况,卖方不在买方按照第 47 条第(1)款规定的额外时间内交付货物,或卖方声明他将不在所规定的时间内交付货物。
(2)但是,如果卖方已交付货物,买方就丧失宣告合同无效的权利,除非:
(a)对于迟延交货,他在知道交货后一段合理时间内这样做;
(b)对于迟延交货以外的任何违反合同的事情:
——他在已知道或理应知道这种违反合同后一段合理时间内这样做;或
——他在买方按照第 47 条第(1)款规定的任何额外时间期满后,或在卖方声明他将不在这一额外时间履行义务后一段合理时间内这样做;或
——他在卖方按照第 48 条第(2)款指明的任何额外时间期满后,或在买方声明他将不接受卖方履行义务后一段合理时间内这样做。

Article 49

(1) The buyer may declare the contract voided:
(a) if the failure by the seller to perform any of his obligations under the contract or this convention amounts to a fundamental breach of contract; or
(b) in case of non-delivery, if the seller does not deliver the goods within the additional period of time fixed by the buyer in accordance with paragraph (1) of article 47 or declares that he will not deliver within the period so fixed.

(2) However, in cases where the seller has delivered the goods, the buyer loses the right to declare the contract voided unless he does so:
(a) in respect of late delivery, within a reasonable time after he has

become aware that delivery has been made;

(b) in respect of any breach other than late delivery, within a reasonable time:

—after he knew or ought to have known of the breach;

—after the expiration of any additional period of time fixed by the buyer in accordance with paragraph (1) of article 47, or after the seller has declared that he will not perform his obligations within such an additional period; or

—after the expiration of any additional period of time indicated by the seller in accordance with paragraph (2) of article 48, or after the buyer has declared that he will not accept performance.

第 50 条

如果货物不符合同，不论价款是否已付，买方都可以减低价格，减价按实际交付的货物在交货时的价值与符合合同的货物在当时的价值两者之间的比例计算。但是，如果卖方按照第 37 条或第 48 条的规定对任何不履行义务做出补救，或者买方拒绝接受卖方按照该两条规定履行义务，则买方不得减低价格。

Article 50

If the goods do not conform with the contract and whether or not the price has already been paid, the buyer may reduce the price in the same proportion as the value that the goods actually delivered had at the time of the delivery bears to the value that conforming goods would have had at that time. However, if the seller remedies any failure to perform his obligations in accordance with article 37 or article 48 or if the buyer refuses to accept performance by the seller in accordance with those articles, the buyer may not reduce the price.

第 51 条

(1)如果卖方只交付一部分货物，或者交付的货物中只有一部分符合合同规定，第 46 条至第 50 条的规定适用于缺漏部分及不符合同规定部分的货物。

(2)买方只有在完全不交付货物或不按照合同规定交付货物等于根本违反合同时，才可以宣告整个合同无效。

Chapter 10   Claims and Arbitration

Article 51

(1) If the seller delivers only a part of the goods or if only a part of the goods delivered is in conformity with the contract, articles 46 to 50 apply in respect of the part which is missing or which does not conform.

(2) The buyer may declare the contract avoided in its entirety only if the failure to make delivery completely or in conformity with the contract amounts to a fundamental breach of the contract.

第 52 条

(1)如果卖方在规定的日期前交付货物,买方可以收取货物,也可以拒绝收取货物。

(2)如果卖方交付的货物数量大于合同规定的数量,买方可以收取也可以拒绝收取多交部分的货物。如果买方收取多交部分货物的全部或一部分,他必须按合同价格付款。

Article 52

(1) If the seller delivers the goods before the date fixed, the buyer may take delivery or refuse to take delivery.

(2) If the seller delivers a quantity of goods greater than that provided for in the contract, the buyer may take delivery or refuse to take delivery of the excess quantity. If the buyer takes delivery of all or part of the excess quantity, he must pay for it at the contract rate.

Exercise

Ⅰ. *Answer short questions*

1. How many ways are there to settle disputes in foreign trade?
2. If disputes arise, what's the first choice?
3. What about the effectiveness of arbitration award? Does it have legal binding force?
4. Which way would people prefer, arbitration or litigation?
5. If one party is from US, the other is from China, can they choose Britain for arbitration?
6. What are the parties called in arbitration?
7. Usually how many arbitrators are there in an arbitral tribunal?

II. True or false statements

1. A contract must be terminated when there is a force majeure event.
2. Settlement of disputes through negotiation is, therefore, even more expensive and complicated than going to the court.
3. The conclusion of the award shall be declared to the parties at the opening session of the hearings.
4. In international trade, the arbitration clause in sales contract should vaguely stipulate the place of arbitration, the organization of arbitration, the applicable arbitration rules and the arbitral award.
5. Force majeure actually means that the frustration of the contract by the party in question results from natural or social forces which include flood, earthquake, typhoon, fire, war and government decrees of prohibition out of the control of mankind.

III. Case study

进出口公司以 CIF 鹿特丹出口食品 1000 箱,即期 L/C 支付。货物装运后,凭已装船清洁 B/L 和已投保的一切险及战争险的保险单,向银行收妥货款。货到目的港后经进口人复检发现以下情况:

(1)该批货物共 10 个批号,抽查 20 箱,发现其中 2 个批号涉及 200 箱含沙门氏细菌超过进口国标准。

(2)收货人实际只收到 998 箱,缺少 2 箱。

(3)有 15 箱货物外表情况良好,但箱内货物共缺少 60 千克。

据此情况,进口人分别向谁索赔?

Glossary

aforesaid	上述的	endorsement	担保
A. R(all risks)	一切险	FAQ(fair average quality)	良好平均品质
arbitral award	仲裁裁决	FAS(free alongside ship)	装运港船边交货
arbitration tribunal	仲裁庭	FCA(free carrier)	货交承运人
acceptance	承兑	file a claim	提出索赔
average	海损	FO(firm offer)	实盘
B/L(Bill of lading)	提单	FOB(free on board)	装运港船上交货
breach of condition	违反要件	force majeure	不可抗力
breach of contract	违约	fortuitous accidents	意外事故
breach of warranty	违反担保	F. P. A	平安险
cash in advance	预付现金	Free in (F. I.)	船方不负责装船费用
carrier	承运人	Free in and out (F. I. O)	船方不负担装卸费用
Chamber of Commerce	商会	Free out(F. O.)	船方不负担卸货费用
charterer	租船人	fundamental breach	根本性违约
confirming bank	保兑行	gallon	加仑
container yard	集装箱堆场	general average	共同海损
convention	公约	GMQ(good merchantable quality)	上好可销品质
counter-offer	还盘	hearings	审理
counter sample	回样	infringement	侵权
cover	承保	Insurance policy	保险单
credit standing	信誉	L/C(letter of credit)	信用证
customs formalities	报关手续	liner transport	班轮运输
default	不履行责任	lighterage	驳运费
defendant	被告	litigation	起诉
discount	贴现	long ton	长吨
discounted proceeds	贴现后的款项	measurement ton	尺码吨
draft	汇票	metric ton	公吨
endorse	背书	more or less clause	溢短装条款

negotiation	议付
negotiable	可转让的
notary public	公证人
offerer	发盘人
offeree	受盘人
onward	（由此）往前
opening bank	开证行
order B/L	指示提单
particular average	单独海损
peril	风险
plaintiff	原告
premium	保险费
quality tolerance	品质公差
right of recourse	追索权
red-clause L/C	红条款信用证
reimbursement	偿付
salvage charge	救助费用
shipping by chartering	租船运输
short ton	短吨
subject matter	标的物
SWIFT (Society for Worldwide Interbank Financial Telecommunications)	环球同业银行金融电信协会
tare	皮重
thereby	因此，从而
T.P.N.D	偷窃提货不着险
trust deed	委托书
trust receipt	信托收据
usance draft	远期汇票
wharfage	码头使用费
W.P.A	水渍险

Reference to Exercise

Chapter 2　Preparation

Ⅰ.

A. 1. 盼望……
2. 有利的答复,佳音
3. 贸易关系的建立
4. 详细情况
5. 目前可供出口的产品
6. 进出口
7. 通函
8. 具体询盘
9. 优惠价格
10. 随附……请查收

B. 1. establish / enter into trade relations
2. prospective buyers / client
3. cotton piece goods
4. business scope
5. at an early date
6. general idea
7. various kinds of
8. price list
9. sample books
10. upon receipt of

Ⅱ.
1. B　2. A　3. B　4. B　5. D　6. B　7. B　8. B　9. A　10. C

Ⅲ.
1. 我们愿意在平等互利的基础上与你公司建立贸易关系。
2. 我们致函,介绍本公司是各种空调的最大的出口商之一。
3. 为了把我们的产品扩展到欧洲市场,我方致函贵方寻求合作机会。
4. 我们有各种各样的颜色和尺寸,能满足多种需求。
5. 我们已经航空邮寄给贵方有关产品的(单页)广告单。如对某些感兴趣,请告知。
6. 经过多年的努力,我们已经拓展了业务范围,目前我们经营近百种产品。
7. 我们主要业务是多种轻工产品的进出口。
8. 万一贵公司不进口上述产品,如能将此信转给相关的公司,我们将非常感激。
9. 作为摩托车出口商,我们愿与贵方在这一行做些交易。
10. 为了让你们大体了解我们的产品,另封寄上目录一份以及三份小册子供贵方参考。

Ⅳ.
1. We are introducing ourselves as an exporter of imitation jewelry with years of experiences in this line.
2. Your letter addressed to our head office last week has been given to us because the article you mentioned falls within our business scope.
3. We have various kinds of light industrial products available for export.
4. We are glad to receive your letter enclosing an illustrated catalogue.

5. We look forward to receiving your specific requirements for our products.
6. We are a well established private company and desire to establish trade relations with you.
7. The manager gave me a brief introduction to Messrs Johnson, which is a prospective customer.
8. In order to give you a general idea of the items in the sheet, we are enclosing a brochure and a latest price list.
9. We consider it as a favorable balance of trade when exports exceed imports.
10. Our products are good in quality and favorable in price.

V.

> Dear Sirs,
>
> We learn from China Daily of last week that you are interested in silk clothes.
>
> We introduce ourselves as a leading exporter here in the line of garments and are willing to set up/establish/enter into business relations with you on the basis of equality and mutual benefit.
>
> Our silk clothes are made of high quality silk materials with traditional workmanship. For your reference, we are enclosing an illustrated catalogue and the latest price list. If you are interested, please send us your specific inquiry on receipt of which we will send our quotation and samples.
>
> We are looking forward to your early reply.
>
> Yours faithfully,
> Jerry

VI.

Date: 20th April, 20...

Foothill Enterprises Trade Development Co., Ltd.

Taiz Street

P. O. Box 22789

Sana'a Republic of Yemen

> Dear Sirs,
>
> Your company has been introduced to us by Commercial Counselor's Office of your embassy in Beijing as prospective buyers of arts & crafts.
>
> In order to introduce our products to the Middle East, we are writing to you in the hope of establishing trade relations.

> The main line of our business covers the export of chinaware of super quality, fashionable design and competitive price, which enjoys a good reputation all over the world. For your information, we are enclosing an illustrated catalogue and the latest. Samples and quotations will be airmailed to you upon receipt of your specific inquiries.
>
> Looking forward to your early reply.
>
> Yours faithfully,
>
> Jerry

Chapter 3 Business Negotiation

Ⅰ.

1. A   2. A   3. ABC   4. ACD   5. A   6. ABCD   7. A   8. ABCD   9. D
10. C   11. D   12. A

Ⅱ.

1. 鉴于你我双方长期的业务关系,我们可以考虑减价。
2. 遗憾地说,你方报价与此地市场行情不一致。
3. 本公司专营纺织品的进口业务。
4. 贵公司已由日本东京商会推荐给我公司。
5. 我们相信通过双方的努力,贸易往来一定会朝着互利的方向发展。
6. 如果贵方能与我方合作,不胜感激。
7. 我们将努力与各国扩大经济合作和技术交流,灵活地运用通常而合理的国际惯例。
8. We regret that it is impossible to accept your counter-offer, even to meet you halfway.
9. In respect of quality, we don't think that the goods of other brands can compare with ours.
10. Our annual requirements for metal fittings are considerable, and we may be able to place substantial orders with you if your prices are competitive and your deliveries are prompt.
11. This offer is subject to the goods being unsold.
12. We have extended the offer as you requested.
13. This offer is based on an expanding market and is competitive.
14. The parties to the contract shall comply with the principle of fairness in defining the rights and obligations of the parties thereto.
15. The parties to the contract shall, in accordance with the principle of good faith, execute the rights and perform the obligations thereof.
16. A commission contract refers to a contract between the commissioning party and the commissioned party whereby the commissioned party shall handle the business of the commissioning party.
17. Shipping advice: The seller shall, immediately upon the completion of the loading of commodity, notify by cable the buyer of the contract number, name of commodity, quantity,

gross weight, invoice value, name of carrying vessel and date of sailing. In case the buyer fails to arrange insurance on time due to the seller's failing to notify by cable, all losses arising therefrom shall be borne by the seller.

Ⅲ.
1. F   2. T   3. F   4. T   5. F   6. T

Ⅳ.
1. Revocation: An offer may be revoked if the revocation reaches the offeree before he has dispatched an acceptance.
2. A non-firm offer is an offer without engagement. It is unclear, incomplete and with reservation.
3. Withdrawal: An offer may be withdrawn if the withdrawal reaches the offeree before or at the same time as the offer.
4. (Omitted)

Ⅴ.
1. No. (omitted)
2. (1)构成发盘。 (2)不成立,是还盘不是接受。 (3)无效。 (4)可以修改发盘,是有效的,4月7日乙方还没有收到信函。 (5)不可撤销。 (6)过了有效期。甲方意图。不成立。 (7)成立。 (8)不成立。 (9)甲方的意图。
3. (Omitted)

Ⅵ.

Dear sirs,

In reply to your letter of/dated April 12 concerning/regarding the chinaware, we are giving an offer, subject to our final confirmation as follows:

Commodity: chinaware

Article Nos.: 512

Price: USD 50 per dozen CIF C 5% Port Sudan

Quantity: 3,400 dozens

Shipment: prompt shipment

Payment: confirmed, irrevocable letter of credit

Under separate cover, we are sending you samples required.

It is known to all that the Chinese chinaware is exquisitely made and moderately priced. It is hoped that you will send us your orders as early as possible.

Yours sincerely,

Jerry

Chapter 4 Quality, Quantity and Packing of Goods

Ⅰ.
1. Fair Average Quality, FAQ
2. 实际皮重、平均皮重、约定皮重、习惯皮重
3. 运输标志、指示性标志、警示性标志
4. 合同价
5. 按品质和按说明
6. 皮重
7. 机动幅度、选择权、超出或不足部分的作价办法
8. 运输包装、销售包装
9. 运输标志、指示性标志、警示性标志
10. 大

Ⅱ.
1. B 2. ABCE 3. C 4. C 5. A 6. E 7. ABCD 8. C 9. B 10. B
11. D 12. C 13. C 14. B 15. B 16. A 17. B 18. B 19. A
20. ABD 21. B 22. ACD 23. ABC 24. ABCD 25. ABCD

Ⅲ.
1. F 2. T 3. F 4. F 5. T 6. F 7. T 8. F 9. F 10. T 11. F
12. T 13. F 14. F

Ⅳ.（略）   Ⅴ.（略）

Chapter 5 Incoterms

Ⅰ.
1. B 2. A 3. D 4. A 5. D 6. A 7. B 8. A 9. C 10. C

Ⅱ.
1. T 2. F 3. F 4. T 5. F 6. T 7. F 8. F

Ⅲ.（略）

Ⅳ.

1. The Freight $=0.2 \times 70 = 14$ USD per case

   And because the CFR C3％ Kuwait price is USD 50.00 per case, then,

   The FOB Shanghai price $=$ CFR $-$ Freight
   $$= \text{CFR C3\%} \times (1-3\%) - 14$$
   $$= 50 \times (1-3\%) - 14$$
   $$= 34.5 \text{ (USD per case)}$$

   i.e. this exporting company should offer FOB Shanghai USD 34.5 per case to its customer with the same profit.

2. 我出口公司从报 CIF 大阪价改为 FOB 大连价时,应将原报价调低,即从原报价中减去货物从大连至大阪的运费和保险费。

   当按 FOB 条件签订合同时,买卖双方除风险的划分没有变化外,他们所承担的责任和费用都发生了变化。按 CIF 大阪条件成交,卖方负责租船订舱和投保,并支付运费和保险费;而改为

FOB大连条件成交时,则由买方派船接货和投保,并支付运费和保险费。

Chapter 6 Ocean Transport

Ⅰ.
1. 记名提单、指示性提单、不记名提单
2. 已装船提单、收妥备运提单
3. 空白抬头、空白背书

Ⅱ.
1. D   2. C   3. C   4. C   5. B   6. C   7. C   8. C   9. B   10. C   11. ABD
12. ABCD   13. ABC   14. BCD

Ⅲ.
1. F   2. F   3. F   4. F   5. F   6. F   7. F   8. F

Ⅳ.（略）

Ⅴ.
1. 商品总重量＝30 千克×1000＝30（公吨）

   商品总体积＝(40×30×20)×1000＝24（立方米）

   ∵总重量＞总体积

   ∴运费＝200×(1＋20％)×30＝7200（港币）

2. 单件体积＝100×40×25＝100 000（立方厘米）＝0.1（立方米）

   单件重量＝95（千克）＝0.095（公吨）

   ∵体积＞重量

   ∴总运费＝80×(1＋10％＋15％)×200＝20 000（美元）

   每件运费为 80×(1＋10％＋15％)＝100（美元）

   CFR 价＝FOB 价＋运费＝400＋100＝500（美元）

   因此,该批货总运费为 20 000 美元,如改报 CFR 价,每件我方可报 500 美元。

Ⅵ.
1. 清洁提单,卖方无责任,可以找船方。   2.（略）   3.（略）

4. The Chinese exporter (seller) hasn't breached the contract provision of "Partial shipment and transshipment are prohibited".

   According to UCP600 "Article 31 Partial Drawings or Shipments", "b. A presentation consisting of more than one set of transport documents evidencing shipment commencing on the same means of conveyance and for the same journey, provided they indicate the same destination, will not be regarded as covering a partial shipment, even if they indicate different dates of shipment or different ports of loading, places of taking in charge or dispatch..."

   In this case, the Chinese exporter shipped the goods on board the same vessel in Shanghai Port and in Guangzhou Port. And then the vessel began to sail to Los Angeles (the same journey). So the Chinese exporter (seller) hasn't breached the contract provision of "Partial shipment and transshipment are prohibited".

Chapter 7　Insurance

Ⅰ.
1. 自然灾害、意外事故
2. 全部损失、部分损失
3. 中国保险条款、平安险、水渍险、一切险
4. 一般附加险、特殊附加险、特别附加险
5. 共同海损、单独海损
6. 施救费用、救助费用
7. 基本险、附加险
8. 平安险、水渍险
9. 仓至仓条款
10. 水上危险
11. 两年

Ⅱ.
1. BCDH　　2. B　　3. C　　4. C　　5. A　　6. A　　7. C　　8. BDE　　9. BDE
10. AB　　11. C　　12. A　　13. C　　14. D　　15. D　　16. D　　17. A　　18. B
19. A　　20. A　　21. D　　22. D　　23. ABCD　　24. BC　　25. ABC　　26. AD

Ⅲ.
1. F　　2. F　　3. F　　4. T　　5. T　　6. T　　7. T　　8. F　　9. F　　10. F　　11. F
12. F　　13. F　　14. T　　15. F　　16. T　　17. T　　18. T　　19. F　　20. F　　21. F

Ⅳ.
1.(1)海上风险包括自然灾害和意外事故两种。
　(2)海上损失是指被保险货物在海运过程中,由于海上风险所造成的损坏或灭失。就货物损失程度来分为全部损失、部分损失。就货物损失的性质部分可分为:共同海损、单独海损。
　(3)外来风险和损失。
2. 共同海损:在海洋途中,船舶、货物或其他财产遭遇共同危险,为了解除共同危险,有意采取合理的救难措施,所直接造成的特殊牺牲和支付的特殊费用。
　单独海损:指仅涉及船舶或货物所有人单方面的利益的损失。
　区别:(1)造成损失的原因不同。(2)涉及的利益方不同。(3)损失承担的方式不同。
3.(略)　　4.(略)
5. 水渍险中不包括由淡水雨淋引起的损失,故保险公司不负有赔偿责任。
6. FOB＝CIF－I－F＝500－500×110％×(2.3％＋5％)－150

Ⅴ.　1.(略)　　2.(略)

Ⅵ.
1. 前者属于单独海损,后者属于共同海损。
2. 推定全损。
3. 平安险;8 件都赔。
4. 第一艘属于自然灾害部分损失,不赔。
　第二艘属于意外事故部分损失,赔。
5. 在码头,未到买方仓库,则保险公司要赔偿,一切险中包括偷窃提货不着险。
6. 100 元,根据平安险的承保范围。
7. 单独海损:船身裂口,水浸货物。

共同海损:修补,抛入海中的货物。
8. (1)单独海损:水渍险,平安险。(2)共同海损:平安险。(3)单独海损:对船投保。
9. 3万:单独海损;8万:共同海损;船:8×100/(100+50+30+8+2)。
10. 保险公司应赔偿。因为根据中国人民保险公司《海运货物保险条款》平安险的责任范围第2条和第3条的规定,触礁受损的8000美元,是运输工具遇到意外事故造成的部分损失,保险公司负责赔偿;遇暴风雨受损的2100美元,是在运输过程中由于自然灾害造成的部分损失,但又因该货物是触礁意外事故发生之前所造成的,所以保险公司对2100美元也该负责赔偿。
11. (1)、(3)是因火灾而造成的直接损失,属单独海损。(2)、(4)、(5)是因维护船、货共同安全,进行灌水灭火而造成的损失和产生的费用,属于共同海损。
12. 保险公司可以拒赔。因为根据"仓至仓"条款规定:保险货物转运时,保险公司的承保责任从开始转运时终止。

Chapter 8 Payment

Ⅰ.
1. C   2. B   3. B   4. B   5. A   6. C   7. B   8. C   9. A   10. C
11. A 12. A 13. B 14. B 15. A 16. B 17. C 18. C 19. AD
20. ABC 21. BCD 22. ABCE 23. ACD 24. ABCD 25. B 26. B
27. B 28. B 29. D 30. A 31. A 32. C 33. D 34. B 35. D
36. D 37. A 38. B 39. B 40. C 41. B 42. B 43. C 44. A
45. C 46. B 47. B 48. B 49. C 50. ABCD

Ⅱ.
1. 错   2. 错   3. 错   4. 对   5. 错   6. 错   7. 错   8. 错   9. 对   10. 对
11. 对 12. 错 13. 错 14. 对 15. 错 16. 错 17. 对 18. 错 19. 错 20. 错

Ⅲ.
信用证:是开证银行对受益人的一种保证,只要受益人履行信用证所规定的条件,即受益人只要提交符合信用证所规定的各种单据,开证行就保证付款,属于银行信用。
循环信用证:规定信用证的金额可以循环使用。
承兑交单:在单据经承兑人承兑后就将单据交付给付款人。
汇票:出票人做出在将来或某确定时间支付给某特定人或来人一定金额的无条件支付命令。
本票:出票人做出在将来或某确定时间支付给某特定人或来人一定金额的无条件支付承诺。
电汇:汇款采用电信的方式。
不可撤销信用证:信用证一经开立后,不经当事人同意,银行不得擅自撤销信用证或更改信用证的有关条款。

Ⅳ. 1. (略)
2. 答:交单日期在提单签发后21天内,同时满足信用证的有效期。
3. (1)答:不合理,因为CIF合同为到货合同。 (2)答:不能。 (3)答:考虑L/C。
4. (略)   5. (略)

Chapter 10 Claims and Arbitration

I.

1. Friendly (amicable) negotiation, arbitration, litigation.
2. Friendly (amicable) negotiation.
3. The decision of the Arbitration Commission shall be final and binding upon both parties; neither party shall seek recourse to a law court nor other authorities to appeal for revision of the decision.
4. Arbitration.
5. Yes.
6. Plaintiff and defendant.
7. Three.

II.

1. F   2. F   3. F   4. F   5. T

III. （略）